NOTO
RIOUS

<u>OTHER BOOKS BY STEVE WILLIAMS</u>

*A Common Sense Approach
to Implementing ISO 2015*

Lean in Plain English

*Modern Hiring: Master the Art of Finding, Evaluating, and Securing
Top Talent for Your Organization (with Dan Beaulieu)*

Quality 101

*Survival Is Not Mandatory: 10 Things
Every CEO Should Know About Lean*

NOTO RIOUS

LEADERSHIP LESSONS FROM HISTORY'S MOST NOTORIOUS LEADERS

STEVE WILLIAMS

atmosphere press

To my soul mate and best friend;
I have loved you all my life.

COVER IMAGE CREDITS:

Image: 00 Me And Sonny.jpg
Source: Wikimedia Commmons
Created by: Wikimedia commons creator - PHIL HM
https://commons.wikimedia.org/wiki/File:00_Me_And_Sonny.jpg
License: Creative Commons Attribution-Share Alike 4.0 International license.

Image: Al Capone in 1930.jpg
Source: Wikimedia Commmons
Created by: Federal Bureau of Investigation employee -
on Wikimedia commons by user: Officer
https://commons.wikimedia.org/wiki/File:Al_Capone_in_1930.jpg
License: public domain

Image: Argunov Catherine the Great.jpg
Source: Wikimedia Commmon
Created by: Ivan Argunov - on Wikimedia commons by user: Artinpl
https://commons.wikimedia.org/wiki/File:Al_Capone_in_1930.jpg
License: public domain -This work is in the public domain in its country of origin
and other countries and areas where the copyright term is the author's life plus
100 years or fewer. This work is in the public domain in the United States because
it was published (or registered with the U.S. Copyright Office) before January 1, 1928

Image: Blackbeard the Pirate (cropped).jpg
Source: Wikimedia Commmon
Created by: Wikimedia commons by user: David Levy
https://commons.wikimedia.org/wiki/File:Blackbeard_the_Pirate_(cropped).jpg
License: public domain - This work is in the public domain in the United States
because it was published (or registered with the U.S. Copyright Office) before
January 1, 1928

Image: Erik le rouge.jpg
Source: Wikimedia Commmon
Created by: Wikimedia commons by user: Ludo29y
https://commons.wikimedia.org/wiki/File:Eugene_Ferdinand_Victor_Delacroix_
Attila_fragment.jpg
License: public domain - {{PD-US}} – US work that is in the public domain in the
US for an unspecified reason, but presumably because it was published in the US
before 1928.

Image: Eugene Ferdinand Victor Delacroix Attila fragment.jpg
Source: Wikimedia Commmon
Created by: Eugène Delacroix - Wikimedia commons by user: Hohum
https://commons.wikimedia.org/wiki/File:Eugene_Ferdinand_Victor_Delacroix_
Attila_fragment.jpg
License: public domain - This work is in the public domain in its country of
origin and other countries and areas where the copyright term is the author's life
plus 100 years or fewer. {{PD-US}} – US work that is in the public domain in the
US for an unspecified reason, but presumably because it was published in the US
before 1928.

Image: Jacques-Louis David - The Emperor Napoleon in His Study at the Tuileries - Google Art Project.jpg
Source: Wikimedia Commmon
Created by: Jacques-Louis David - Wikimedia commons by user: DcoetzeeBot
https://commons.wikimedia.org/wiki/File:Jacques-Louis_David_-_The_Emperor_Napoleon_in_His_Study_at_the_Tuileries_-_Google_Art_Project.jpg
License: public domain - This work is in the public domain in its country of origin and other countries and areas where the copyright term is the author's life plus 100 years or fewer This work is in the public domain in the United States because it was published (or registered with the U.S. Copyright Office) before January 1, 1928.

Image: File: YuanEmperorAlbumGenghisPortrait.jpg
Source: Wikimedia Commmon
Created by: Wikimedia commons by user: Kcx36
https://commons.wikimedia.org/wiki/File:YuanEmperorAlbumGenghisPortrait.jpg
License: public domain - This work is in the public domain in its country of origin and other countries and areas where the copyright term is the author's life plus 100 years or fewer This work is in the public domain in the United States because it was published (or registered with the U.S. Copyright Office) before January 1, 1928.

Image: File: Steve Jobs in 1972 Pegasus.jpg
Source: Wikimedia Commmon
Created by: Wikimedia commons by user: FunnyMath
https://commons.wikimedia.org/wiki/File:Steve_Jobs_in_1972_Pegasus.jpg
License: public domain - This work is in the public domain in the United States because it was published in the United States between 1928 and 1977, inclusive, without a copyright notice. For further explanation, see Commons:Hirtle chart as well as a detailed definition of "publication" for public art. Note that it may still be copyrighted in jurisdictions that do not apply the rule of the shorter term for US works (depending on the date of the author's death), such as Canada (50 p.m.a.), Mainland China (50 p.m.a., not Hong Kong or Macao), Germany (70 p.m.a.), Mexico (100 p.m.a.), Switzerland (70 p.m.a.), and other countries with individual treaties.

Image: File: 吴司马孙武.jpg
Source: Wikimedia Commmon
Created by: Wikimedia commons by user: Taiwania Justo
https://commons.wikimedia.org/wiki/File:吴司马孙武.jpg
License: public domain - This work is in the public domain in the United States because it was published (or registered with the U.S. Copyright Office) before January 1, 1928.

Image: File: An Icelandic woman in her bridal dress - Drawings from Sir Joseph Banks' Voyage to the Hebrides, Orkneys, and Iceland (1772), No.17 - BL Add MS 15512.jpg
Source: Wikimedia Commmon
Created by: John Clovelly - Wikimedia commons by user: Jheald
https://commons.wikimedia.org/wiki/File:An_Icelandic_woman_in_her_bridal_dress_-_Drawings_from_Sir_Joseph_Banks%27_Voyage_to_the_Hebrides,_Orkneys,_and_Iceland_(1772),_No.17_-_BL_Add_MS_15512.jpg

Image: File: Williams Cover Photo
Created by: Kara Reese Photography

INTERIOR ILLUSTRATION CREDIT:

All illustrations created by: Natasha Lyn (Wier) Lehndorf

FOREWORD

I have just finished reading a fascinating book titled *Notorious: Leadership Lessons from History's Most Notorious Leaders* by management consultant and author Steve Williams. When I first picked it up, I was intrigued that he decided to write a book about some of the most notorious leaders throughout history. When I'm reviewing a book for someone whom I want to have on my show, and I've heard the book is good, I kind of skim through it. But with *Notorious*, I kept turning the pages and turning the pages, and the next thing I knew, I was done.

I learned so much because you think you know who these people are because you've heard their names from television or history books you have read but you don't think of them in this context. You just think Genghis Khan had 80,000 soldiers and he did all the "notorious" things you have heard, but then you read this book and learn he had to be a pretty good leader to be able to pull that off.

The book makes us think about what we can learn from Genghis and the others in the book. I found it fascinating that all these people throughout history had another side; I don't think they were teaching their secrets at the Wharton Business School, so we don't know this side of them. The lessons in *Notorious* are all so valuable and entertaining that I just read right through the book and couldn't put it down.

Interestingly, I had been watching the *Vikings: Valhalla* show, and then all of a sudden, bam, Freydis was in it! I had just finished *Notorious* and there she was in the show, Freydis Eiriksdottir, and she was portrayed just as in the book and I thought, wow, I know that about her because of *Notorious*.

So, bottom line, *Notorious* is totally unique and I highly rec-
ommend it and encourage people to read the book.

Jack Canfield

TABLE OF CONTENTS

SUN TZU

ON TALENT MANAGEMENT
544–496 BC

Born Sun Wu in 544 BC but later bestowed the honorific name of Sun Tzu, which means "Master Sun," Sun Tzu was a Chinese military general, strategist, and philosopher who ruled in the sixth century BC of ancient China. He is most widely known as the author of *The Art of War*, an extremely influential ancient Chinese book on military strategy that had a significant impact on Chinese warfare, culture, and history. *The Art of War*, is a treatise on military strategy and tactics. It explores various aspects of warfare, including the importance of planning, understanding the enemy, exploiting strengths and weaknesses, and achieving victory with minimal conflict. *The Art of War* has been generally accepted as a masterpiece on strategy, frequently cited and referred to by military generals and theorists since the time it was first published to the modern day. It has been studied and applied not only in military contexts but also in fields like business, politics, and sports. Tzu's *Art of War* strategy was based on five governing factors:

1. **THE MORAL LAW:** Loyalty of his followers regardless of the danger.

2. **HEAVEN:** Providing the environmental conditions surrounding battle.

3. **EARTH:** Compromises the danger or safety of traveling great distances.

4. **THE COMMANDER:** The virtues of wisdom, benevolence, and courage.

5. **METHOD AND DISCIPLINE:** The proper rule of the armies, including tactical plans, logistics, and expenditures.

One of the few surviving historical stories of Sun Tzu is as follows:

After writing The Art of War, Sun Tzu got an audience with the king of Wu. The king invited him to demonstrate his military skills by training the court concubines. Sun Tzu accepted the challenge.

Sun Tzu explained the commands for marching, but when the drum signals were given, the women burst out laughing. Sun Tzu teaches that if the orders are not clear, the general is at fault. So he repeated his explanation, but the women only laughed again. Sun Tzu teaches that when the orders are clear but not followed, the officers are at fault. So Sun Tzu ordered the women's commanders, the king's two favorite concubines, beheaded.

After the two were executed and replaced, the remaining women obeyed the orders precisely. The king was too sickened by the deaths to watch the demonstrations, but he gave Sun Tzu command of his army.

Sun Tzu said, "In the practical art of war, the best thing of all is to take the enemy's country whole and intact; to shatter and destroy it is not so good. So, too, it is better to recapture an army entire than to destroy it, to capture a regiment, a detachment, or a company entire than to destroy them." His first option was to be smarter than his opponent, not more violent. He also understood the value of converting the general population of his enemies into subjects instead of destroying them; this benevolent approach added exponentially to his empire while promoting appreciation and loyalty. Sun Tzu's *Art of War* principles have been utilized throughout time in both the military arena and the business world to build creative, successful strategies.

LESSON 1:

DEVELOP POTENTIAL LEADERS

"Leadership is a matter of intelligence, trustworthiness,
humaneness, courage, and sternness."
– Sun Tzu

Sun Tzu's timeless book *The Art of War*, established Tzu as a magnificent military mind and expert in wartime tactics and strategy. One of the things that makes Tzu special is that he recognized that, as good as he was, he couldn't do it alone. He would need to develop a stable of highly competent generals to lead Tzu's soldiers and execute his plans. Tzu had a clear set of attributes that he would use to develop and train his potential generals.

Sun Tzu emphasized the importance of leaders having a deep understanding of their domain. Leaders should continuously develop their knowledge and skills relevant to their field of expertise. These skills either came from prior experience and/or Sun Tzu's leadership teachings. His leaders would need to possess the necessary technical and strategic expertise to effectively guide their teams.

Sun Tzu was ahead of his time in many areas, one of which was recognizing the significance of self-awareness in leadership. He knew that effective leaders understand their strengths, weaknesses, and biases. They actively reflect on their actions and continuously strive for self-improvement. By understanding themselves, leaders can better understand and relate to their team members.

Sun Tzu emphasized the importance of strategic thinking and planning in his teachings. His leaders would need to develop their ability to analyze complex situations, anticipate challenges, and formulate effective strategies. They should be able to identify opportunities and risks, make informed decisions, and effectively allocate resources in executing his military plans.

Sun Tzu acknowledged the value of communication and influence in leadership. Effective leaders should develop strong communication skills, both verbal and nonverbal, to clearly convey their vision, goals, and expectations to their teams. They should inspire and motivate others, build relationships, and influence stakeholders to support their initiatives.

Sun Tzu recognized the need for his generals to be adaptable and agile in response to changing circumstances. He felt that effective leaders should be open to new ideas, willing to challenge the status quo, and able to adjust their strategies when necessary. They should embrace change, foster a culture of innovation, and encourage creative problem-solving.

A key aspect of Sun Tzu's leadership development plans was based on promoting from within through mentorship and developing others with potential. Many of his top leaders were "homegrown," meaning that Tzu would have to train these green officers in his philosophies and tactics on war and conflict. He demanded that his generals mentor and coach the next generation of leaders who would join the veterans in battle, helping them develop their skills and capabilities. Tzu knew that he needed to have strong bench strength and felt developing the potential of others would ensure an ongoing strong and capable team.

Sun Tzu stressed the significance of leading by example,

embodying the values, behaviors, and work ethic he expected from his teams. On a day-to-day basis, he demonstrated integrity, professionalism, and a commitment to excellence that was infectious. Tzu set a very high bar that few could match, but with Tzu's training and personal teachings, they could come close. By setting a positive example, leaders inspire their teams to strive for greatness.

LESSONS IN ACTION

"When EF Hutton speaks, people listen." Anyone within a couple of decades of my age remembers this tagline from the ubiquitous commercials of the '70s and '80s for the EF Hutton stock brokerage. Fifty years later it still sticks with me. An important leadership lesson is that real leaders are not just at the C-level executive offices, leaders can be found at all levels of an organization. In some cases, the official leader has the title but does not have the attitude, personality, or talent to get others to follow. On the other hand, there are informal leaders in every organization, and while they don't have the title, they are often more effective leaders than the ones that do.

I was with a client recently and this "grassroots leadership" was on full display. When I am speaking or teaching, I have the unique perspective of being able to watch the audience and observe behaviors and reactions to what I am saying. I was recently facilitating an ISO certification Kickoff meeting with a group of shop supervisors and department leads at a new client. We had about fifteen people in the room, including the operations manager. I was feeling pretty good about my communication skills as I saw a sea of nodding heads as I was speaking. One woman, Sally, nodded enthusiastically after something brilliant I had obviously just said, but then I noticed a very slight delay before others began to also nod. As I continued to talk, it became clear that many in the room were taking their cues from Sally, and not necessarily from my charismatic dialogue. When I asked the team if they were ready for the level of commitment, support, and work the project required, most of them looked first to Sally and not the operations manager before verbally agreeing.

It was clear that Sally was the "real leader" on the shop floor, the one everyone looked to for help and guidance. While this is not the norm, nor should it be, there are informal leaders in every company. Positional leaders have a title but not always a following, while real leaders have a following but not always a title. Positional leaders influence positionally, while real leaders influence everyone. How do you become a real leader? Real leaders become real leaders because of the following traits.

Character refers to the qualities, values, and traits that define and shape a leader's behavior, decision-making, and interactions with others. It encompasses a leader's moral compass, integrity, and the principles they uphold. Leadership character is essential for inspiring trust, guiding ethical decision-making, and promoting the well-being of the team or organization.

Leaders form relationships and connections with their team members, colleagues, stakeholders, and other individuals within an organization or community. These relationships are essential for effective leadership and can greatly impact the success and performance of a team or organization.

The collective wisdom, insights, and information passed down within a particular group or organization through informal channels, typically from experienced individuals to newer members, is tribal knowledge. It consists of practical knowledge, best practices, unwritten rules, and lessons learned that are not typically documented or formalized.

The ability of leaders to make decisions and judgments based on their gut feelings, instincts, or a deep understanding of a situation, even in the absence of complete information or logical reasoning. It involves relying on one's inner sense or "knowing" to guide decision-making and actions.

The practical knowledge, skills, and insights gained by individuals through their real-world involvement in leadership roles or responsibilities. It encompasses the lessons learned, successes achieved, challenges faced, and growth experienced while leading others and managing various aspects of an organization or team.

Remember: The title does not make the leader; the leader makes the title.

TAKEAWAYS

Recognize leadership potential. Look for employees that work hard, take initiative, and own their responsibilities. These three attributes are a good predictor of advancement potential.

Monitor failure. How an employee responds to failures and setbacks, particularly when it wasn't their fault, will reveal how they might react to adversity as a leader.

Consider personality. Skills can be trained, personality cannot and will only be magnified in a leadership position. Half of the employees that leave a company are leaving the leader and not the job.

Be a mentor. The fastest way to achieve your goals is to help others achieve theirs. Sharing your experience and expertise allows the mentee to develop their leadership skills while under your direct guidance.

LESSON 2

BUILD HIGH-IMPACT TEAMS

"When the common soldiers are too strong and their officers too weak, the result is insubordination. When the officers are too strong and the common soldiers too weak, the result is collapse."
– Sun Tzu

Sun Tzu believed that a leader's success depends on the quality of their team. Leaders should focus on building cohesive teams, fostering a sense of unity and trust, and nurturing the talents and abilities of their team members. Collaboration and effective communication are key components of successful teamwork. If you think of any military force, they are made up of many teams (platoons, battalions, squadrons, etc.). Sun Tzu's teachings on building teams primarily revolve around selecting capable individuals, fostering a strong team culture, and maximizing the collective strengths of the team members. What follows are examples of how Sun Tzu applied his principles to building wartime teams.

Sun Tzu emphasized the importance of selecting the right individuals for a team. He advocated for assessing the skills, experience, and character of potential team members to ensure they are capable and aligned with the team's objectives. This involves evaluating their strengths, weaknesses, and potential contributions to the team.

Building a strong team involves selecting the right individuals and developing their skills. Identify the strengths and expertise required for the team's success. When recruiting, consider individuals who complement each other's skills and can work well together. Provide opportunities for training, mentorship, and professional development to enhance individual and team capabilities.

Effective team building requires strong leadership, and Sun Tzu demonstrated this principle with the dominant military teams he built. Leaders should inspire and motivate team members, provide guidance, and make timely decisions. They should also create an environment of trust and open communication, encouraging collaboration and idea sharing among team members.

Sun Tzu stressed the importance of creating a cohesive team culture built on trust, respect, and shared values. He believed that a strong team culture encourages loyalty, commitment, and collaboration among team members.

Sun Tzu understood that leveraging the unique strengths and talents of individual team members would maximize the team's overall capabilities. He believed that by recognizing and utilizing each team member's strengths, the team becomes stronger as a whole.

Sun Tzu taught the importance of clear and effective communication to ensure coordination and synchronization within a team. He believed that open communication enables the team to respond quickly and effectively to changes and challenges.

Teams must be adaptable and flexible to navigate changing circumstances. Encourage team members to be agile and responsive to emerging challenges or new information. Foster a culture that values creativity, problem-solving, and continuous improvement.

Sun Tzu's principles are timeless; leaders in any business can build strong and effective teams that are capable, cohesive, and adaptable. Sun Tzu's teachings provide valuable insights into team-building strategies that can help leaders create high-performing teams capable of achieving their objectives.

LESSONS IN ACTION

One of the most powerful tools in the operational leadership toolbox is not something you can put your hands around but, if mastered, can take organizational performance to a new level. Highly effective teams can make the difference between step function improvement and abject failure.

Group dynamics, simply stated, are the forces at work that affect how individuals interact in a team environment based on such things as their experiences, culture, personality, and social skills. Providing formal group dynamics and team-building training to an organization's management will increase the effectiveness of any team. The most important role is that of the facilitator; a highly skilled facilitator will make or break any team. Thus, developing a core of highly skilled facilitators is a critical task to maximize the power of teams for any organization. Depending on the task at hand, teams have a wide variety of needs, and members should be selected to fill the appropriate roles. Put any group of people together for any length of time and you quickly begin to see individuals assuming various roles naturally. But when structuring a team to accomplish a particular task, highly effective teams are the ones in which the roles have been matched with particular member strengths during the selection process.

When I was teaching for the MBA program and now when doing leadership development training, I do the following exercise as soon as we finish introductions on day one. There are typically anywhere from eight to twelve participants in the training, and I pass out "roles" for each of them to play during the exercise. The assignment for the group is to come up with a list within twenty minutes of ten things that are critical in some aspect of the organization. Each item on the list must be unanimous or it doesn't make the list. One of the roles is the Facilitator, who has complete control of running the meeting any way they want. Some of the other roles include Dominator, Brown Noser, Naysayer, Digresser, and Feuding Rivals. Of course, these roles are engineered to create conflict and make creating a solid list difficult.

After we debriefed, I explained that the purpose of the exercise was to expose some of the personalities the leaders will observe in a team setting. While all of these personalities may not be in the same meeting, I guarantee that one or more will be present in most meetings. The lesson here is to be able to identify these roles and manage each in a way that will maximize the team's effectiveness. Since personality has a significant effect on individual behavior, it is magnified in the team environment and will ultimately determine the level of effectiveness that the team can achieve. Meshing diverse personalities can be a challenge, but that is where synergy can come into play again. While having a "devil's advocate" member can be extremely beneficial, members with an overly negative or low level of "agreeableness" can disrupt and erode team cohesiveness and not make model team members.

In any team environment, I will put the following up on the whiteboard and ask what I mean by "1+1=3." Other than the suggestion that I am the product of the public school system, I usually get a bunch of blank stares. My point in this can be answered by the ancient saying "two heads are better than one" or synergy. Synergy is the phenomenon in which the efforts of a group will result in a performance that is greater than the sum of the individual inputs. Barring severe time, money, etc. constraints, a properly assembled and functional team will usually make a better decision than a single individual. The varying perspectives, experiences, and cultures the members bring to the table not only facilitate alternate solutions, but also provide a check and balance for individual biases.

A note on conflict: Conflict is an unavoidable part of human nature and inevitable in a team environment. Not all conflict is bad, and how conflict is managed determines whether it will be constructive or destructive. A properly functioning team will need a certain degree of constructive conflict to stimulate creative thinking and avoid complacency. Often people want to avoid conflict if at all possible, but if handled well, conflict can be positive, constructive, and, I would argue, necessary.

How to be effective in a team environment is a learned behavior and not one without its challenges. Overcoming individual resistance, managing the influence of cultural differences, and replacing individual achievement with a team environment are some of the major obstacles to success. However, team members can be shaped through group dynamics and team-building training, properly matching employees to roles, and retooling the reward system to encourage cooperative efforts. A skilled facilitator can guide individual strengths and talents into the proper channels. Putting it all together, understanding group dynamics can be a powerful tool for developing highly effective teams in any organization.

TAKEAWAYS

Build a dream team. Getting the right people on the bus is not good enough, you need to get the right people on the bus and in the right seat.

Embrace diversity. Weak leaders build a team with people that share the leader's views while great leaders build their teams with people that will challenge the leader's views.

Match strengths to tasks. Nothing sabotages a team quicker than assigning a role that doesn't match the person's strengths. Understand the strengths and weaknesses of each team member and assign roles accordingly.

Establish accountability. Define the purpose and goal of the team and clearly assign accountability to each member based on responsibilities. If done right, the team will self-monitor underperformers without intervention from the leader.

ATTILA THE HUN

ON LEADING FEARLESSLY
406-453

Born in what is now Hungary circa 406, Attila the Hun was the fifth-century king of the Hunnic Empire and one of history's most fearless rulers. His name means "Little Father," and it is unclear whether this was his birth name, as it is highly speculated it was conferred on him as a tribute of respect and adoration by his followers. This name conferred with affection would come to be synonymous with terror among his enemies and the territories his armies conquered. He devastated the lands from the Black Sea to the Mediterranean, inspiring fear throughout the late Roman Empire. Dubbed "Flagellum Dei" (Scourge of God), Attila's rise to power occurred after the death of his uncle, Rugila, who had co-ruled the Huns alongside Attila's father. Following Rugila's death, Attila and his twin brother, Bleda, whom Attila called Buda, assumed joint leadership of the Hunnic Empire. Attila was the military half and Buda was the diplomatic half of the brothers' rule. Attila felt his brother was always getting in his way and considered him a pest. He also felt that his brother was too passive to be a ruler, and when

Buda negotiated a peace agreement with the Roman Empire, Attila had him murdered on a hunting trip. This also cleared the way for the greedy Attila to assume sole leadership of the Hunnic Empire. Legend has it that Attila felt so guilty over this that he named a city on the Danube after his brother, Budapest.

Attila was a much more aggressive ruler than his brother and boldly attacked the Eastern Roman Empire despite the peace agreement Buda had negotiated. Attila expanded the rule of the Huns to include many Germanic tribes and boldly attacked the Eastern Roman Empire. His invasions that drove the German populations through the borders of the Western Roman Empire, were a significant contributor to the eventual fall of Rome. Attila's armies were often a mixture of various tribes, and his ability to command these diverse warriors with an iron fist gave him a competitive advantage over the Roman generals, who had great difficulty keeping control of their non-Roman fighters, across the battle lines. Attila was notorious for his fierce gaze and took delight in the terror it inspired. He also perpetuated this image by claiming to own the actual sword of Mars, the Roman god of war. One of history's first charismatic leaders, Attila was a brilliant military leader with a commanding presence that held his empire together through the strength of his personality.

Attila had multiple wives throughout his life, most of which were political marriages that expanded his control. Attila the Hun died mysteriously on his wedding night in 453 at the age of forty-seven. There has been much speculation over the cause of his death, but there are three accounts that are discussed more than any other. One is that he may have overindulged after his marriage to Ildico, with a wedding night of excessive food and alcohol. He reportedly went to bed, and on the following day, it appeared that he had choked on his blood after a nosebleed. The second account says he experienced a brain hemorrhage or liver damage from his lifestyle. Finally, some believe that Ildico killed her husband as she was the last to see him alive in a plot with Marcian, a rival emperor of the East. We'll never know the truth of Attila's death as it remains unsolved.

LESSON 3

BE DECISIVE
IN YOUR ACTIONS

"It takes less courage to criticize the decisions of others
than to stand by your own."
– Attila the Hun

Attila the Hun ruled with a strong hand and expected unwavering loyalty from his subordinates. He made his expectations clear and demanded obedience and dedication from his followers. Attila's firm leadership style instilled a sense of discipline and decisiveness among his troops, enabling them to execute his orders effectively. He demonstrated his decisiveness through various aspects of his leadership and military campaigns. Attila had the ability to make quick decisions, especially in critical situations. Whether it was choosing the target of his next invasion, altering battle strategies on the spot, or capitalizing on his enemies' weaknesses, Attila didn't hesitate to act. His ability to assess situations rapidly and make firm choices allowed him to maintain the initiative and keep his opponents off-balance.

Attila had a clear vision of expanding the Hunnic Empire and was unwavering in his pursuit of conquest. He made decisive plans to invade territories, often taking advantage of political instability or conflicts among rival powers. Attila didn't waste time deliberating excessively, but swiftly mobilized his forces and launched expeditions, relentlessly pushing the boundaries of his empire. Attila was not only decisive in his overall objectives but also adaptable in his strategies. He recognized the importance of adapting to changing circumstances and adjusting his plans accordingly. Attila could swiftly modify his tactics based on the terrain, the strength of his enemies, or unexpected developments on the battlefield. This flexibility allowed him to exploit opportunities and overcome obstacles. Attila was known for his audacious and daring military tactics; he didn't shy away from taking risks and was willing to make bold moves to gain an advantage. Whether it was splitting his forces, launching surprise attacks, or executing flanking maneuvers, Attila's decisive actions on the battlefield often caught his adversaries off guard and led to significant victories. Attila the Hun's decisiveness was perfectly illustrated in two famous historical battles during his invasion of France, the Siege of Metz, and the Battle of Châlons.

THE SIEGE OF METZ

During Attila's invasion of Gaul (modern-day France) in 451, he besieged the city of Metz. The Roman general, Aetius, along with his allies, was preparing to confront Attila's forces. Sensing the imminent threat, the citizens of Metz requested Aetius to come to their aid. However, Aetius was hesitant to engage in battle and kept delaying his arrival, causing anxiety among the citizens and defenders of Metz. In this critical situation, Attila recognized the indecisiveness of his opponent, saw an opportunity, and decided to take decisive action. Realizing that Aetius was not coming to rescue the city, Attila launched a full-scale assault on Metz. The Huns attacked with such ferocity and determination that the defenders of Metz were overwhelmed, and the city fell to Attila's forces. This victory demonstrated Attila's ability to seize opportunities and make quick decisions in the face of uncertainty.

THE BATTLE OF CHÂLONS

In 451, Attila faced a coalition of Roman and Visigothic forces led by Aetius at the Battle of Châlons in Gaul. Attila recognized the strategic importance of this battle and understood that its outcome would significantly impact his conquest of Western Europe. During the battle, as the fighting raged on, Attila observed the Roman and Visigothic lines holding strong against his forces. Realizing that his chances of victory were diminishing, Attila made a decisive and daring move. He ordered a contingent of his cavalry to ride around the battlefield and attack the rear of the enemy lines, creating confusion and disarray among his opponents. Attila's unexpected maneuver caught the Roman and Visigothic forces off guard, leading to chaos and disruption in their ranks. This turning point allowed the Huns to gain the upper hand and ultimately emerge victorious. Attila's ability to adapt his strategy mid battle and make a bold decision helped secure his triumph at the Battle of Châlons.

These aspects of Attila the Hun's leadership demonstrate his decisiveness as a military leader. He possessed the ability to make quick decisions, adapt to changing circumstances, and employ bold tactics to achieve his objectives. Attila's decisive nature played a crucial role in his successes as he relentlessly pursued his ambitions and expanded the Hunnic Empire.

LESSONS IN ACTION

One of the core competencies of a great leader is the ability to be decisive in their decision-making. This means having the confidence to weigh the available information against the situation, swiftly make a decision, and stand by it. Confidence comes from experience in similar situations, the resulting decisions, and the results of those decisions (both good and bad). Do great leaders always make the right decisions? Of course not, but just as much can be learned from the wrong decisions as the right ones. Every decision a leader makes is closely watched by the people they lead as well as the leader's conviction in that decision. Nothing erodes trust faster than a wishy-washy leader who just cannot seem to make a definitive decision. Now, while leaders may not always make the right choice, those whose bad decisions outnumber their good ones will never rise to become great leaders and, in fact, probably won't remain any kind of leader very long.

Decisiveness is not a leadership skill I had to develop; from early in my career, making a decision was never something I struggled with. What did take some time to appreciate was the part about "weighing the available information against the situation" before making the decision, including seeking input from others involved and impacted by the decision. That lesson took years and, numerous dubious decisions on my part, to be ingrained into my decision-making process. That being said, no amount of data, analysis, reports, or projections will decide for you. While I fully believe in the adage that the best predictor of future behavior is past behavior, all the data comes from looking backward. Decision effectiveness is based on what will happen in the future and leaders need to be able to extrapolate historical results into the current situation and evaluate the proper course to take, which may not align with past decisions. Leaders understand that they will never be 100 percent sure it is the correct decision until after it has been made and the results become available. For the life of that decision, it will be attributed to the person who made the decision, and this requires a willingness to take risks and pure courage. In today's highly disruptive environment, decisions need to be made quickly to maintain competitive advantages.

Given that even the greatest leaders will occasionally make a bad decision, another aspect of courage is the ability to recognize poor decisions and quickly change course. The natural tendency of insecure leaders is to defend their bad decisions, but taking too long to recognize a poor decision can negatively influence the perception of an individual's effectiveness. To paraphrase my good friend Dr. Phil: "The only thing worse than making a bad decision is sticking with a bad decision."

A note on "Paralysis by Analysis.": This is both a complicated yet simple axiom that speaks to the need to be able to adapt and make decisions using the best information available at the time. There is a very fine line between rushing to judgment and postponing a decision to wait for endless amounts of data, and not every leader possesses the ability to distinguish between the two. What truly distinguishes a great leader from the rest is the ability to make a great decision with incomplete information. This is where a high level of leadership skill is critical to determine the cost-benefit analysis of waiting for more information versus the need to do something right now. To quote another of my mentors, General George S. Patton, "A good plan violently executed now is better than a perfect plan executed next week."

TAKEAWAYS

Be boldly decisive. It is better to risk being wrong than to delay too long and be right. Deliberate with caution, but act with decision.

Resist the urge to second-guess. Learn to trust your instincts; better decisions are generally made by following your gut than by overthinking the issue; studies show a 90 percent success rate of decisions based on intuition.

Never fear failure. Good decisions are the result of experience, experience is the result of bad decisions. Accept that you will occasionally make mistakes and learn from them.

Imperfect information is the norm; deal with it. Perfect information is only available when a 100 percent accurate prediction can be made about the future. Use the best information available in the moment and quickly act upon it.

LESSON 4

NEGOTIATE WIN-WINS

"I, Attila, gather you in this council to enlighten you as to how to conduct yourself at those times when you will be required to negotiate for the good of your Huns and tribes and perhaps our nation. The techniques of negotiation are not easily taught. It is for both Hun and chieftain to learn skills useful in negotiating. These are mastered only through understanding gained by experience."
– Attila the Hun

The following two examples illustrate that Attila the Hun was not entirely impervious to negotiation or diplomatic engagements. However, it's important to note that his negotiations were often driven by his military might and the strategic advantage he held. Attila's primary focus remained on expanding his empire and extracting tribute from the territories he conquered.

In 452, Attila and his Hunnic forces were advancing through Italy, causing fear and panic among the Roman population. As the Huns approached Rome, Pope Leo I took it upon himself to negotiate with Attila and prevent the destruction of the city. According to historical accounts, Pope Leo I, accompanied by a small group of clergymen, met Attila and his army on the outskirts of Rome. Attila, known for his ferocity and disregard for diplomacy, was surprised by the pope's presence and treated him with respect. The details of the negotiation between Attila and Pope Leo I are not well documented, but it is believed that the pope used a combination of diplomatic skills, appeals to Attila's religious beliefs, and possibly a promise of payment to persuade Attila to spare Rome. This would come to be known as "The Meeting of the Two Powers."

It is said that the pope convinced Attila by invoking the memory of St. Peter, claiming that the apostle would protect the city from destruction. To the surprise of many, Attila agreed to spare Rome and abruptly withdrew his forces. The exact reasons behind his decision remain uncertain, but it is believed that the pope's negotiation skills and the fear of divine retribution played a significant role. This encounter between Attila the Hun and Pope Leo I demonstrated the importance of diplomacy and negotiation even in the face of seemingly unstoppable military forces. The event also highlighted Attila's willingness to negotiate under specific circumstances, showcasing a more nuanced side to his character beyond his reputation as a brutal conqueror.

In 449, Attila initiated negotiations with the Eastern Roman Empire, led by Emperor Theodosius II. Attila had previously raided the Eastern Roman territories, and Theodosius II sought to establish a more stable relationship. The negotiations resulted in the signing of the Peace of Anatolius (also known as the Treaty of Margus) later that year. The treaty was named after the Roman general, Flavius Anatolius, who acted as a negotiator on behalf of the Eastern Roman Empire. The Peace of Anatolius was aimed at ending the hostilities and establishing a more stable relationship between the Huns and the Eastern Roman Empire. The terms of the treaty included a substantial annual tribute to be paid to Attila by the Eastern Roman Empire. This tribute was likely a form of protection money and acknowledgment of Attila's dominance and military power. This peace agreement helped stabilize the eastern frontier and temporarily halted Attila's military campaigns in that region.

Attila understood that not all victories could be won with brute force; many conflicts required finesse and the power of the mind. The same is true in today's business environment; you can certainly win the battle with an opponent by wielding the hammer when you have leverage, but the war will be won and long-term relationships forged by negotiating as many win-win agreements as possible. It is said that to be a great leader you have to want to be in charge, and Attila did.

LESSONS IN ACTION

Everything in life is a negotiation. However, if you ask ten people if they think they are good negotiators you are likely to get around eight that answer no. Let that sink in; if everything in life is a negotiation, wouldn't you expect most people to be good at it? The reason many automatically answer no can usually be traced back to an uncomfortable and/or unpleasant experience negotiating something like a new vehicle. All the back-and-forth gamesmanship on price and the tiresome charade of "I need to run your offer by my manager" can certainly leave a bad taste in anyone's mouth. But in terms of root-cause analysis, that experience is only the symptom, not the root cause. Negotiation is a process and a skill that needs to be practiced and honed before it can be repeatedly performed successfully. In the context of this lesson, success is defined as negotiating a win-win result, as opposed to a zero-sum result. Everyone walks away from the table satisfied with the result, while a zero-sum means there is one winner and one loser. The winning party in this scenario may have won the battle with their opponent, but may very well lose the war in future exchanges with that party. The true root cause of most people's aversion to negotiating is a lack of process training in the art of negotiation.

I was an adjunct professor for a dozen years, teaching for the MBA program at several universities in the evenings. One of my favorite class exercises was on the topic of negotiation in my Organizational Behavior courses. Before the exercise, I would always ask the class how many thought they were good negotiators, and the results from dozens of classes support the earlier statement that roughly 80 percent of people will answer no. Many, many years ago I was fortunate to train with Chester L. Karrass, the globally acknowledged foremost expert on negotiation. The title of one of his many books says it all, *In Business As In Life, You Don't Get What You Deserve, You Get What You Negotiate.* Anyone who doubts this need only reflect on any conversation they have had with a young child! Let's explore the process of negotiation.

There are five stages of negotiation: Preparation and Planning, Relationship-Building, Information Exchange, Bargaining, and Agreement.

Preparation and Planning: Perhaps the most mission-critical of the five stages, researching both sides of the discussion to identify any possible trade-offs, determining your most desired and least desired possible outcomes, and setting ground rules. Making a strategic list of what concessions you're willing to put on the bargaining table comes next; a very successful technique is to start with small concessions that may be more important to your opponent with the hope they will pave the way to larger concessions important to you. The final preparation step is critical; prepare your BATNA, the Best Alternative to a Negotiated Agreement.

A win-win provides both parties with a solution equally satisfying. When a win-win negotiation breaks down, BATNA is the next best outcome for both sides. If both sides have determined their most desired and least desired outcomes, there should be an area of overlap between the two. For example, if one party is selling an item for $100 but would take $80, and the buyer would like to buy the item for $70 but would go as high as $90, the ZOPA or Zone of Potential Agreement would be $80-$90. Anywhere within this $10 settlement range would give both parties some of what they want.

Relationship-Building: Relationships matter in business, and negotiations are no different. Strong relationships between negotiating parties tend to end with better results, period. To build a long-term relationship in negotiations, work collaboratively and build agreements that benefit both sides, especially if it's likely both sides will be working together over time. At the negotiation table, the best way to uncover your negotiation counterpart's hidden interests is by building a relationship, asking questions, and listening carefully.

Information Exchange: This stage occurs when you begin to engage the other side, share information, and explore options and interests. The focus should be on what you each need as opposed to negotiating positions. The trick here is to decide how much of your hand to show and what to hide without giving away too much information before the bargaining even starts. Rushing through this stage and jumping straight into negotiating will make you seem hasty and give the other side an unearned advantage. This will form the foundation for what you each ask for later in the Bargaining Stage.

Bargaining Stage: This stage is the meat of the process of negotiation, during which both sides begin an iterative exercise of give-and-take. After the initial first offer, each negotiating party should propose different counteroffers while keeping in mind and managing their concessions. During the bargaining process, emotions must be kept in check; the best negotiators use strong verbal communication skills of active listening, calm feedback, and in face-to-face negotiation, this also includes body language. The goal of this step is to emerge with a win-win outcome, a positive result for both sides.

Agreement: Once an acceptable solution has been agreed upon, both sides should thank each other for the discussion, no matter the outcome of the negotiation; remember, successful negotiations are all about creating and maintaining good long-term relationships. The expectations of each party should be clearly outlined and, preferably, documented with a written agreement. This step eliminates ambiguity and clearly outlines the position of each party that can be enforced if one party doesn't live up to their end of the bargain.

For the exercises, I would pair up the students and provide one with a buyer's sheet and the other with a seller's sheet for an item such as a bicycle. Each sheet had a story reflecting their side of the negotiation and enough information to allow everyone to prepare their strategy and determine their most and least desirable positions. The stories also had incentives for reaching a settlement as well as penalties for failing. They were free to embellish their stories and use any strategy they wished, but it was clearly understood that if a solution or BATNA was not reached, neither party would benefit at all. They were given time to develop their strategy and hone their story, and then the negotiating would begin. After the training on the negotiation process and hands-on exercises, I would ask the class if anyone felt better about their skills. Virtually 100 percent would say their negotiating skills had improved and felt more comfortable in these situations.

TAKEAWAYS

Do your homework. The fastest way to be on the wrong end of a zero-sum agreement is to walk in unprepared. Never leave negotiation to luck; part of your preparation is to fully understand your opponent's strengths and weaknesses.

Honor all commitments. Follow through on the commitments you make during negotiations; failure to do so will create distrust in the future. You will likely be back at the table with them on other issues.

Know your opponent's "must haves." When doing your homework, it is essential to get a feel for what the other side needs to reach agreement. Knowledge is leverage, and negotiating is all about leverage.

Concede the little stuff. Make early concessions on things that are unimportant to you, but show your willingness to negotiate to the other party. This will make it easier to hold firm on the big stuff.

FREYDIS EIRIKSDOTTIR

ON LEADING FROM THE FRONT
975-UNKNOWN

Freydis Eiriksdottir was born in Iceland in 975 into one of the most feared Norse bloodlines of the time. Her father was the infamous Viking, Erik the Red, and her older half brother was Leif Erikson. Freydis was the illegitimate daughter of Erik the Red, a product of an affair by her father, and the name of Freydis's birth mother is still unknown to this day. She had a relatively uneventful childhood, growing up in the same household with her father and Leif and her two half brothers, Thorstein and Thorvald. In their early years, Leif and Freydis developed a close bond that lasted throughout their lives, fighting many battles side by side. Growing up in this environment, Eiriksdottir defied the expectations of her gender as she grew into a woman of strong character who was more fearless than even the most celebrated male Vikings. While not as well-known as their male counterparts in print, film, and legend, there were Viking Shield-Maidens who were every bit the warrior as the men. While her father and brother were legitimate badass Vikings, little sister Freydis was a true warrior with an insane, vengeful penchant for slaughtering her enemies with an axe that would have brought a tear of joy to her father's cheek.

Eiriksdottir married very young to a wealthy but frail man (by Viking standards) called Thorvard. She became a brutal warrior who would accompany her husband and brother on their sailing expeditions. Although brutal, violent, and extremely power hungry, Freydis was a very brave and resourceful woman, paving the way for other Norsewomen to become warriors and command their own ships. With her flaming red hair, fearless attitude, and bigger-than-life presence, Freydis became a symbol of the Viking way to both male and female warriors. An interesting historical note: Freydis was credited with inventing an early form of the sleeping bag on one of her voyages by fashioning the ship's sail into somewhat of a cocoon for warmth and sleeping. The date of Eiriksdottir's death is unknown, but surprisingly it is thought that she lived to a ripe old age and died of natural causes. While Freydis's expedition to Vinland did not result in a long-lasting Norse presence in North America, her role in the saga reflects her strong personality and assertiveness. Her actions and reputation have made her a notable figure in Viking history and the exploration of North America during that era.

Freydis Eiriksdottir is a very controversial historical figure; some accounts portray her as a hero, a strong-willed woman, and a fearless warrior, while others describe her as a deranged murderess. I will leave it up to you to decide for yourself; I tend to believe she was probably a little of both.

LESSON 5

WALK THE WALK

---

*"Why do you flee from such pitiful wretches, brave men like you?
You should be able to slaughter them like cattle! If I had a weapon,
I am sure I could fight better than any of you!"*
– Freydis Eiriksdottir

Freydis Eiriksdottir was a woman who was driven by profit, adventure, and at times greed and anger. The above quote was shouted in defiance to her expedition party that was retreating from an enemy attack. As the daughter of Erik the Red, Freydis was exposed to the rugged and independent lifestyle of Viking explorers, which formed the early foundation of her leadership qualities. Watching her father gain unflinching loyalty from his crews by following through on his promises, showing consistency between his actions and words, and actively engaging in behaviors that aligned with his beliefs, Freydis learned firsthand the importance of walking the walk. She became familiar with the challenges and risks associated with living in harsh environments and sailing across treacherous seas. It is possible that she learned essential skills such as navigation, sailing, and survival techniques from her father and other members of the Viking community.

Freydis had begun joining her brother, Leif, on his expeditions to observe, learn, and gain on-the-job experience. Eiriksdottir gained her first notoriety in 1004 while on an expedition to the New World led by Thorfinn Karlsefni. With three ships and 160 Vikings, they set off, but the journey was extremely harsh with violent storms and a lack of food. During the voyage, tensions arose between Freydis and her crew. Freydis, known for her strong-willed and assertive nature, clashed with her fellow explorers, leading to a breakdown in relations. Despite these conflicts, the expedition arrived in Vinland and established a temporary settlement on the east coast of North America (present-day Canada) to begin what would become a three-year excursion. The Vikings quickly developed a trade agreement with the local Native Americans and traded peacefully for the first year.

Later, while negotiating a trade with the natives for food and dairy products, a fight broke out and Freydis's party retreated. Freydis, determined to protect their interests and resources, tried to follow the men, but since she was pregnant, she soon began to fall behind and lose sight of them. She ran past the body of a fallen comrade slain by a blow to the head with a rock and then saw the natives preparing to follow the Viking party armed with rocks and stones. As they pursued the Vikings, the natives suddenly came across Freydis and surrounded her. Fearlessly, she seized hold of the fallen Viking's sword, opened her tunic to reveal one of her breasts, and beat the sword against it while letting loose a blood-curdling war cry. The natives fled in terror as they thought that since their enemy had left but a single, pregnant woman screaming indecipherable obscenities to fight them all, she must have some sort of magical power.

LESSONS IN ACTION

To "walk the walk" means to demonstrate through actions and behaviors the values, principles, and qualities that a leader espouses.

It involves aligning one's words with their deeds and setting an example for others to follow. Leaders should embody the behaviors and qualities they expect from their team members. Whether it's integrity, accountability, or dedication, they should consistently demonstrate these attributes in their actions. Fortunately, this is one of the few leadership lessons I didn't have to learn. It must have been present in my leadership DNA from the beginning.

They say you never forget your first, and I will always remember the first time I led an organization to ISO certification. *ISO 9000* was published in 1987 and is an international standard for quality management systems (QMS). It took quite a while for it to be embraced by American companies and become the ubiquitous baseline for quality that it is today. As the top quality executive for a multi-plant manufacturing company in the mid-1990s, I was tasked with building a QMS from the ground up and achieving ISO certification within twelve months, an expedited implementation at the time. For a company with no knowledge of ISO and with no current system in place, meeting this deadline was significant. When we had the project kickoff, I committed to the workforce that we would achieve this milestone and that I would be working side by side with them along the way. By making this promise, I knew I had to back it up with my actions, coaching, and rolling up my sleeves. What follows are several key activities that demonstrated to the workforce that I would keep my promise to them.

Communicating clearly was critically important to articulating my vision, goals, and expectations clearly and consistently. This clarity would help everyone, from the cleaning personnel to the president understand what was expected of them and enable them to align their actions accordingly. Frequent communication related to the QMS would become an ongoing activity and new normal for the company.

Practicing active listening with the various team members to quickly address questions or guidance when they didn't understand something. The leadership team had to collectively foster an environment where everyone felt heard and valued.

By demonstrating genuine interest and empathy, leaders can build trust and create a culture of open communication.

Promoting a positive culture as a leader had a significant impact on how the organization or team embraced and integrated the culture into their daily activities. There were highs and lows during this project, and reinforcing a positive environment got us through the lows. By promoting teamwork, collaboration, respect, and inclusivity, we created an environment where individuals felt motivated and empowered to do their best work.

Making tough decisions is something leaders should not shy away from, especially when the decision is not a popular one. This includes addressing performance issues, resolving conflicts, or making unpopular choices. By demonstrating courage and decisiveness, leaders gain respect and build trust among their team members. Tough decisions became a daily event with this project as we taught everyone to abandon their way of life and learn new ways of doing their jobs

Establishing autonomous teams was the foundation for assuring a successful initiative, so the first thing I did was establish an ISO Steering Committee comprised of the Leadership Team members of each functional process in the company. As the name suggests, this team was responsible for oversight of the project and, later, the performance of the company. Together, we next created teams that we called PIT Crews (Process Improvement Teams) and weekly meetings. These teams were departmentally based and made up of people from the appropriate department and led by the department supervisor. There was also a representative from quality and the ISO Steering Committee on each team for support and guidance, but not to direct the team.

Recognizing and rewarding achievements is a core skill that leaders need to develop to acknowledge and appreciate the contributions and success of their team members. Recognizing their efforts publicly and providing meaningful rewards or incentives significantly fostered a positive and motivated work environment. This was addressed in a couple of ways at both the individual and team levels. At the individual level, I established a monthly ISO Rally that was an all-hands-on-deck meeting where we reviewed the status of the QMS. Employees would also be quizzed on ISO requirements and were rewarded with a company ISO shirt with our quality policy on it. Employees really wanted those shirts, and it also represented their pride in their contribution. At the team level, we established performance goals for the PIT Crews, and if they hit the goals for three consecutive months, the supervisor would take the department out for a lunch on the company. This was also greatly appreciated and fostered teamwork.

Continuously developing the leaders on the team turned them into lifelong learners who would actively seek opportunities to improve their knowledge, skills, and leadership capabilities. By investing in their development, the leaders inspired their team members to do the same. It proved important to communicate that we, as leaders, do not have all the answers and are learning as much from the workforce as they were learning from us.

Staying true to core values allowed the leaders to uphold their core values even in challenging situations. They remained consistent in their decision-making and avoided compromising their principles. By staying true to their values, the leaders inspired trust and integrity in their teams. I believe that I had kept my promise to the employees and stayed true to the goals we set in the kickoff meeting. The project was a total success as we became the first company in our industry to become ISO-certified in the state. What we accomplished together would be a source of pride for us all the rest of our lives.

Remember, "walking the walk" is an ongoing process. It requires leaders to be authentic, self-aware, and committed to continuous improvement. By consistently demonstrating their values and principles through actions, leaders can inspire and motivate their team members to do the same.

TAKEAWAYS

Tell them, then show them. True leaders walk the walk while poor leaders only talk the talk. Most people will talk the talk, few will walk the walk; be one of the few.

Be flawlessly consistent. Consistency is crucial in demonstrating integrity. Ensure that your actions are in line with your words consistently over time. Avoid contradictions or hypocrisy that might undermine your credibility.

Keep your promises, always. Promises made, promises kept should become your mantra. Nothing erodes confidence in a leader faster than breaking a promise.

Be accountable. Not only to yourself, but also be accountable to those you lead. Take responsibility for your actions and their consequences. If you make a mistake, admit it and work to rectify the situation.

LESSON 6

LEAD BY EXAMPLE

"Hand me an axe."
– Freydis Eiriksdottir

Freydis was not only a commanding leader but also led by example. During many bloody confrontations, she fought fiercely and fearlessly, inspiring her crew to follow her lead. Her willingness to physically engage in combat demonstrated her bravery and dedication, reinforcing her position as a leader. Freydis was known for her independent nature, and while she was part of her father Erik the Red's legacy, she asserted her authority and independence during three expeditions to Vinland (present-day Newfoundland). Her actions and decision-making showed a desire for autonomy and the ability to lead the way.

Around 1010 Freydis Eiriksdottir set out on a journey from Gardar to meet with two brothers, Helgi and Finnbogi, to propose that they all make the journey to Vinland on their two ships and have a half share of any profits from it. The brothers agreed and Freydis, along with her husband Thorvard, joined an expedition to Vinland led by her brother, Leif Erikson, and Thorvald Erikson. According to the agreement between Freydis and the two brothers, each was to bring thirty fighting men plus their women aboard his ship. Not trusting the brothers, Freydis secretly took five extra men, concealing them so that the brothers were not aware of them until they had reached Vinland. During their time in Vinland, conflicts and tensions arose within the Norse group. A breakdown in trust and unity among the members resulted, which ultimately led to a division between Freydis and her husband on one side and brothers Helgi and Finnbogi on the other. The conflict centered around a specific incident in which Helgi and Finnbogi discovered a hidden treasure in Vinland. They decided to keep it a secret from the rest of the group, including Freydis and Thorvard.

When Freydis eventually discovered their secret, she became enraged and demanded a share of the treasure. When they were unable to agree, the situation escalated into violence and Freydis and her supporters attacked Helgi and Finnbogi, leading to their deaths. Soon all the men had been killed and only the women were left as no one would kill them. Frustrated with her men's unwillingness to dispatch the women, Freydis uttered her infamous request, "Hand me an axe." She then attacked the five women, killing them all. Freydis never hesitated to fight side by side with her crew from the frontline.

Freydis proved many times that she could become a ruthless and vengeful warrior who would not hesitate to use violence to protect her interests and assert her authority. Violence would become Freydis's preferred conflict resolution technique. The story of Freydis, Helgi, and Finnbogi is a significant part of the Vinland sagas, highlighting the conflicts and tensions that arose during the Norse exploration of North America. It emphasizes Freydis's assertiveness and her willingness to take extreme measures to ensure her power and control over situations.

LESSONS IN ACTION

While the context of Freydis's request for the axe was rather gruesome, the underlying principle is to never ask your employees to do something you are not willing to do yourself. This classic leadership lesson is just as valid today as it was over 1,000 years ago; people will follow a leader who is not only on the battlefield with them but out in front of the troops. Freydis understood leading by example would inspire her people to willingly follow her into Hell if she asked them to. Her natural leadership style of being on the frontline inspired this loyalty. Ask yourself whom you would rather work for, a boss that barks out orders from the isolation of the corner office he never leaves or the boss that rolls up her sleeves on the factory floor, working with you to solve problems? While violence and fear were certainly a major component of the Viking culture, respect for their leaders was the hallmark of the legendary ones. Leading from behind just won't work, whether with a team of engineers, factory workers, family—or a group of Vikings.

I am sure that everyone remembers the childhood phrase "Monkey see, monkey do" and when boiled down this is exactly what it means to walk the walk. The tendency of people to mimic the behaviors of their leaders is a very basic aspect of human nature. When a leader demonstrates behaviors that lead to success, people follow. But the same is true when a leader demonstrates bad behaviors. So, how do you take measure of yourself? A good, honest assessment of ourselves is the starting point to understanding how others see us. Ask yourself the following questions:

Do I . . .

- **Know my values and the message I want to project?**

- **Live my message and lead by example?**

- **Walk the walk?**

- **Do what's right, not what's easy?**

- **Know my people and communicate on their level?**

- **Place integrity over expedience?**

- **Believe in others?**

- **Offer direction and hope?**

- **And the most important question: "Would I want me as a boss?"**

These are all required attributes of a great leader, and if you answered "No" to any of the above questions, you have a roadmap for your leadership development. You might even want to consult a colleague (family and friends may be biased) for an independent assessment of where your actions don't match up with your values. Your colleague might be calling your baby ugly, but this feedback must be taken in a constructive way and without getting defensive. One of the leadership training exercises I do is to ask the participants to make a list of their perceived leadership qualities. I tuck that away for the time being and during a later session I ask the same group to make a list of the qualities they would like to see in their employees: integrity, loyalty, work ethic, whatever they may be. Then we compare the two lists, which is usually an eye-opening event for some of them as there are always several attributes that don't match.

Monkey see, monkey do.

Many people have it backward, which is the fundamental reason they fail. They believe that if the cause is good enough, people will automatically buy-in and follow. But with apologies to my friend Kevin Costner, it doesn't work that way. People don't follow worthy causes; they follow worthy leaders. People buy-into the leader first, then the leader's vision.

> ## TAKEAWAYS
>
> **Go first.** You can't lead others farther than you have gone yourself. Remember, you are always defined by your actions, not your words.
>
> **Set the bar high.** Leading by example always works. Set a positive standard for others to follow and demonstrate the behaviors and qualities you expect from them.
>
> **Act with integrity.** People are inspired by leaders who have strong moral character and demonstrate integrity in their actions. Be honest, transparent, and trustworthy in your interactions.
>
> **Inspire others through your actions.** Be authentic; when you stay true to who you are and act in alignment with your principles, you inspire others to do the same.

GENGHIS KHAN

ON SUPERIOR TACTICS
1162-1227

Born Temüjin (meaning "iron") in 1162, Mongol leader Genghis Khan rose from humble beginnings to become what many have called the greatest war tactician of all time. He was born clutching a blood clot in his fist, a traditional Mongol sign that he was destined to become a great leader; however, his early path would be full of tragedy and obstacles. His father, Yesukhei, had kidnapped his mother, Hoelun, and forced her into marriage. At the tender age of nine, his father arranged a marriage for him and sent Khan to live with his future wife, Borte, and her family.

Following the death of his father at the hands of a former ally, the Tartar tribe, he returned home to claim his father's position as clan chief. However, the clan rejected the young, inexperienced Khan, and all but banished the family into a life of poverty. This experience would stay with Khan for the rest of his life and become the driving force in his rise to power. During this time, his mother taught him many of the survival skills that would serve him well throughout his reign. It was then that Khan began his lifelong journey as a student of tribal warfare. He was captured during a raid in

1177, but later escaped and formed his first fighting unit comprised of his brothers and several clansmen. A year later, his wife was kidnapped to become the chieftain's wife in a rival tribe. Khan assembled a fighting force of 20,000 men and was able to rescue her. Together they had four sons and an unknown number of daughters.

It was then that Genghis Khan began his rise to power through an unconventional strategy: destroy the divisions among the various nomadic tribes and unite the Mongols under his rule. His first order of business was to destroy the Tatar army and avenge his father's death. After uniting the nomadic tribes of Mongolia to create the most advanced professional army ever seen in Asia, Khan developed the largest land empire in history by conquering huge chunks of central Asia and China. After several crushing victories, tribal leaders bestowed on Temüjin the honorific title Genghis Khan, which means "Universal Ruler." This title carried not only military significance, but the leading shaman declared Genghis Khan to be the spiritual representative of Mongke Koko Tengri, the supreme god of the Mongols.

The popular belief in academic circles has long been that Genghis Khan was so evil, unwashed, and cold-blooded that there is nothing that can be learned from him. I would strongly argue that the popular belief is wrong—dead wrong—and would go so far as to say that most of the "popular belief rhetoric" about him was just flat-out misinformation. Genghis Khan was truly a leader well ahead of his time in terms of his ideology and leadership style. Most people will be shocked to learn that Genghis Khan:

- Abolished torture.

- Loathed aristocratic privilege.

- Granted religious freedom to his subjects.

- Ran his kingdoms based on merit (a kind of twelfth-century "pay for performance").

- Advanced women's rights in Mongol society.

- Was a lifelong learner.

- Encouraged trade.

- Created the first international postal system.

At their peak, the Mongols controlled 11-12 million contiguous square miles, an area about the size of Africa. The Mongol army owed their domination to the brilliant military tactics of Genghis Khan, as well as his seemingly supernatural anticipation of his enemies' tactics. The well-trained army was also well equipped with each warrior carrying a bow and arrows, shield, dagger, and a lasso. They also carried large waterproof saddlebags for food, tools, and spare clothes, and which could be inflated to serve as a life preserver when crossing deep and swift-moving waters. While Genghis Khan's invasions were brutal in terms of loss of life, the previously mentioned social reforms Khan implemented enriched the quality of life for his subjects and moved the Mongol culture forward. Genghis Khan died in 1227 during a military campaign against the Chinese kingdom of Xi Xia, allegedly falling off his horse and dying from internal injuries at age sixty-five. His final resting place remains unknown.

LESSON 7

SHATTER THE STATUS QUO

---

*"Just as God gave different fingers to the hand, so has
He given different ways to men."*
– Genghis Khan

Genghis Kahn truly was "one of the greatest military strategists to combine technology and cunning warfare tactics to out-think his enemies. Psychological warfare was one of the many tools Khan used to gain an advantage. Because he was so feared, opponents often surrendered before the battle began. This was no accident; a standard tactic was to send out scouts to determine the strength of the opponent and to spread stories of Genghis Khan's violent conquests to instill the belief that no one stood a chance against the Mongol army. When traveling, the warriors would drag large objects behind their horses to create dust storms and would burn hundreds of extra fires at night. This would create the perception that his advancing troops were much more numerous than they were. Mongol soldiers drilled small holes in their arrows to make them whistle while in flight, which was intended to terrify the enemy.

Another path where Khan separated himself from his contemporaries is how he dealt with his enemies. Kahn was not afraid to learn from his competition; when a conquest was made, he would meet with the senior members of the opponent to debrief on their strategies and tactics and would adopt the ones that improved his army. He was extremely intelligent and would execute devious but brilliant battle plans that his opponents would not be able to overcome. Khan employed an extensive spy network and was quick to adopt new technologies from his enemies. The well-trained Mongol fighters coordinated their advance with a sophisticated signaling system of smoke and burning torches. Large drums sounded commands to charge, and further orders were conveyed with flag signals. All soldiers were equipped with a small sword, a javelin, body armor, a battle ax or mace, and a lance with a hook to pull enemies off their horses.

The Mongols were devastating in their attacks and Kahn's military tactics showcased his superiority in warfare. Because they could maneuver a galloping horse using only their legs, their hands were free to shoot arrows. Horses were the biggest asset of the Mongol army and were revered and well taken care of. Each warrior had four to six horses and would rotate them with each day's campaign to ensure that no one horse was ridden to exhaustion. This greatly enhanced the Mongol army's mobility. They could and did travel great distances, often covering sixty to one hundred miles in a day. Because of this unheard-of mobility, no other army could match them.

Another particularly effective tactic Kahn liked to use was the feigned withdrawal: while in the middle of battle, he would often order his troops to withdraw, pretending to have accepted defeat. As the enemy forces moved in for the kill, they would quickly realize that they had walked right into an ambush as hidden detachments of well-armored men would suddenly appear and overwhelm them. To ensure the well-oiled operation of the army, Khan provided an equally well-organized supply system of oxcarts carrying food, military equipment, shamans for spiritual and medical aid, and officials to catalog the spoils of the raids.

LESSONS IN ACTION

Great leaders all have a common trait that separates them from the good, the bad, and the ugly that make up the rest of the leadership continuum: critical thinking. Critical thinkers constantly challenge the status quo and refuse to accept the typical pushback of "well, that's the way it has always been done." Challenging the status quo is a rare but essential trait in business. Why? Because it's hard, really hard. Going along to get along is familiar and comfortable and often deeply ingrained in organizational culture. People are creatures of habit, and basic human nature dictates that people will typically be uncomfortable with change. Companies often get stuck in an innovation rut because no one is willing to rock the boat, either from fear of change or acceptance of complacency.

Exceptional leaders not only have the strength and confidence to shatter the status quo but also the ability to inspire others to buy-into the vision with unshakable loyalty.

I use this lesson with every one of my clients. One of the core offerings of my consulting business is improving operational performance by improving their business process. When working with a new client, I challenge them to bust out of the "This is the way we have always done it" mentality as we work through the business management system (BMS). Together we deep dive into every process, from quoting through shipping, to answer four questions:

1. How is this process currently being performed?

2. Why are we doing it this way?

3. Are all the things we are doing adding value to the organization?

4. Is there a better way to do this? Anything that is not adding value should be eliminated; for things

that are working, let's find a way to streamline and improve them.

One of my favorite management consultants is Tom Peters, author of the In Search of Excellence book franchise. When attending one of his appearances in the early '80s, Peters made a statement that stuck with me throughout my career. When talking about hiring leaders, he said: "If you are looking for a needle mover, never hire a 4.0." It wasn't until I was well into my leadership journey that I began to understand and embrace this advice. What Tom was talking about was that people who strive to be perfect don't color outside the lines. They follow the rules and don't think outside the box; in other words, they live in the status quo. Now don't get me wrong, the 4.0s are critical to running a successful business, but they are not the visionaries that will bust through the status quo and lead the organization to bigger and better things.

I lived this point while in my undergrad program. I was caught up in the whole "perfection" ideal and wanted to finish with a 4.0 GPA. I was a typical Type A overachiever, but along with that came the stress and pressure to be perfect. About halfway through, I received my first B, taking the 4.0 goal off the table. Once that happened, it was like a bolder was lifted off my shoulders and I was able to enjoy the process. This was a critical revelation that was instrumental later while balancing my MBA, work, and family. I now gladly embrace my "perfect imperfection."

TAKEAWAYS

Be a leader, not a manager. The manager accepts the status quo; the leader challenges it and drives creative destruction.

Don't hire a 4.0 if you are looking for a needle mover. While 4.0s are essential to running a successful business they are not the visionaries that will bust through the status quo. The status quo has never produced any game changers.

Acknowledge there will be resistance to change. Leaders don't limit their challenges; they challenge their limits. Persistence and results will quickly overcome the naysayers.

Create a culture of disruption. Innovation is the key to "future-proofing" and should be encouraged and celebrated.

LESSON 8

BUILDING THE RIGHT TEAM

"Those who were adept and brave fellows I have made military commanders. Those who were quick and nimble I have made herders of horses. Those who were not adept I have given a small whip and sent to be shepherds."
– Genghis Khan

While Genghis Khan would often brutally murder and slaughter his opponents, many of his best generals and field commanders came from conquered enemies. As his empire grew, he often sought the opinions of conquered Chinese leaders who had perfected the bureaucracy required to efficiently run a large empire. Khan would not hesitate to consider plans suggested by his former enemies if they provided an advantage over traditional Mongol tactics. He was very keen at identifying the strengths and weaknesses of his personnel and placing them in positions that would maximize their potential, whether it was for a command position, field leader, or a general soldier. Khan was a master at building relationships with all levels of his community and army, and he also had the unique leadership ability to convert the most valuable captured enemy leaders into loyal followers.

Management theory in the twentieth century was consumed

with finding the magic number of employees that any one manager could effectively oversee. Over 800 years earlier, Genghis Khan may have been the first leader to understand the concept of "span of control" and apply it in his military operation. He organized his teams based on the principle of ten. His army was divided into units of ten, a hundred, a thousand, and ten thousand, with the leader of each tier reporting to the next level up. Khan would develop a close personal relationship with the leaders of the units of ten thousand, who would report directly to him. That kind of loyalty was extremely important in his rise to power and in his ability to maintain authority over all the various segments of his domain. As the opening quote illustrated, Khan was also skilled at recognizing the skills, strengths, and weaknesses of his warriors and fitting them into a position that best capitalized on their strengths and minimized their weaknesses.

LESSONS IN ACTION

Many businesses develop tunnel vision that their internal strategies are the only way and are resistant to believe that their competition may be smarter than they are. A related characteristic of this is the trait that insecure managers share of not wanting to transfer their knowledge and experience to their followers for fear of their jobs. The other key element to this point is to play to the strengths of your team; don't force a person into a role that they are not suited for; instead, success will be maximized by finding a role that fits both a person's strengths and weaknesses.

The ability to create high-performing teams is one of the most powerful tools in the operational improvement toolbox. It is not something you can touch and feel but, if mastered, can take organizational performance to a new level. Highly effective teams can make the difference between step function improvement and abject failure. Group dynamics, simply stated, are the forces at work that affect how individuals interact in a team environment, based on such things as their experiences, culture, personality, and social skills. There is a direct correlation between group dynamics and operational improvement, and teams are arguably the most effective vehicle available to an organization.

As a John Maxwell certified leadership coach, trainer, and speaker I frequently get requests for leadership development training. The common problem stated by the owner or president behind closed doors is, "My leadership team is so dysfunctional they can't even work together, much less lead the company. I need help to transform them into a highly functioning team." I have found that in most cases the members don't dislike each other but don't know how to work with the diverse personalities of the others.

During the first session, I will put the following up on the whiteboard and ask what I mean by "1+1=3." Other than the suggestion that I am a product of the public school system, I usually get a bunch of blank stares. My point in this can be answered by the ancient saying "two heads are better than one" or synergy. Barring severe time, money, etc. constraints, a properly assembled and functional team will usually make a better decision than a single individual. I then administer the Myers-Briggs Personality Type test to everyone and we review the results together. I put a matrix on the board with the sixteen personality types and place each member's name in their corresponding box. Each type indicates how that type likes to take in information from others and how they like to communicate with others.

Simply understanding their propensities and how they may conflict with another team member is always eye-opening. Once they recognize these two aspects, they can appreciate why there has been friction with certain other leaders. Once this is crystal clear, we move on to the meat of the leadership training. So, how do you start creating high-performing teams? There are four basic concepts to developing effective teams: Context, Composition, Work Design, and Process.

1. The four contextual factors most significantly correlated to team performance are the presence of adequate resources, effective team leadership, an environment of trust, and a reward system that recognizes team achievements. A key aspect is adequate resources, which begins with senior management and includes time, proper equipment, staffing, and information.

2. Composition includes all the attributes related to actually staffing the team. Matching the required tasks to individual abilities is key and includes both technical and problem-solving skills. Other factors include Personality, Allocating Roles, Diversity, and Team Size. Diversity in terms of gender, age, education, personality, functional specialization, and experience will lead to fresh ideas and perspectives. In general terms, the optimal team size is five to seven; less than four limits the diversity of thought and greater than nine becomes dysfunctional.

3. Work Design encompasses how the team will function (i.e., how much freedom, autonomy, and authority the team has). Empowering teams with decision-making authority will motivate the members and maximize team effectiveness.

4. The process relates to the establishment of team objectives, and as with most objectives, it is highly recommended to use the SMART acronym: Specific, Measurable, Attainable, Realistic, and Timely.

How to be effective in a team environment is a learned behavior and not one without its challenges. Overcoming individual resistance, managing the influence of cultural differences, and replacing individual achievement with a team environment are some of the major obstacles to success. However, team members can be shaped through group dynamics and team-building training, properly matching employees to roles, and retooling the reward system to encourage cooperative efforts. A skilled facilitator can guide individual strengths and talents into the proper channels. Putting it all together, understanding group dynamics can be a powerful tool for developing highly effective teams in any organization.

TAKEAWAYS

Hire people smarter than you whenever you can. Don't be afraid to hire the competition, and learn from them. Covet employees that want your job; the shortest path for them is to make you successful.

Seek people with a learning attitude. This is simply a self-initiated, voluntary attitude that comes from natural curiosity and motivation It is binary, either they have it or they don't.

Do your homework and due diligence. It is far more costly to fire the wrong person than to hire the right one. A new hire is the most important decision you will make all year.

Don't underestimate the importance of culture fit. Skills can be trained but personality, passion, and attitude cannot.

BLACKBEARD THE PIRATE

ON BRANDING
1680-1718

Edward "Blackbeard" Teach was born in the town of Bristol in 1680, a town on the Avon River in southwest England that had produced several pirates. Not much is known about his early years, but Teach began his pirate education when he served on a privateer; an armed ship hired by the British government to attack the ships of the enemy during the War of the Spanish Succession. In the early 1700s, Blackbeard joined the pirate crew of Captain Benjamin Hornigold, who operated off the coast of North America. Blackbeard quickly gained a reputation for his fearsome appearance and ruthless tactics. After Hornigold retired from piracy, Blackbeard took command of his ship, the *Queen Anne's Revenge*, which he captured and refitted for piracy. He became known for his audacious attacks on merchant vessels and his ability to strike fear into the hearts of his victims.

Blackbeard's preferred method of attack was to intimidate his targets into surrendering without a fight, but he was quick to resort to violence when necessary. Blackbeard's autocratic leadership style was truly old school, and it had to be to lead a group of the most merciless and violent criminals to ever band together on the high seas. Ruling with an iron fist demanded equal amounts of respect and fear among his followers, and Blackbeard commanded both. While one of the most feared pirates of his time, his reign of fear was relatively short but intense as Blackbeard and his crew of pirates terrorized sailors from 1716 through 1718. He operated primarily in the waters of the West Indies, targeting ships along the eastern coast of the American colonies and the Caribbean. His activities brought him into conflict with colonial authorities, who saw him as a significant threat to their economic interests.

In November 1718, a force led by Lieutenant Robert Maynard of the Royal Navy engaged Blackbeard's crew in a fierce battle off the coast of North Carolina. The pirate had relatively few men, as most of his men were on shore at the time. He almost got away, and although he fought fiercely, in the end, the thirty-eight-year-old pirate was killed in hand-to-hand combat on the deck of his ship. When Blackbeard's body was later examined, it was found to have five bullet wounds and twenty sword cuts from the fight. Following his death, Maynard's men decapitated Blackbeard and hung his head from the bowsprit of their ship as a gruesome trophy. Before the final battle, one of his crew had asked Blackbeard if his wife knew where his treasure was buried. Blackbeard bellowed, "Only the Devil and I know the whereabouts of my treasure, and the one of us that lives the longest should take it all." To this day, Blackbeard's treasure has never been found.

During his short reign, Blackbeard established himself as one of the most notorious pirates of his time, and his legend has endured long after his death. Stories and myths surrounding his exploits have been embellished and romanticized over the centuries, contributing to his status as one of the most iconic pirates in history. His name is often associated with the stereotypical image of a fearsome and cunning pirate captain.

LESSON 9

CULTIVATE YOUR BRAND

---

*"A pirate, just like a normal person, would probably rather
not have killed someone, but pirates knew that if that person
resisted them and they didn't do something about it, their
reputation and thus their brand name would be impaired."*
– Peter Leeson on Blackbeard the Pirate

Blackbeard became the most cunning and feared pirate to sail
the West Indies, and this reputation was strategically crafted
as he became known for his violent nature. He would often
engage in brutal acts of piracy, including plundering ships, loot-
ing coastal towns, and engaging in violent confrontations with
his enemies. These actions earned him a reputation as a merciless and dangerous pirate. Blackbeard was also an astute tactician who used his knowledge of naval warfare to his advantage.
He would often employ surprise attacks and ambushes, using
his superior firepower to overpower his adversaries. His strategic approach to piracy added to his reputation as a formidable
opponent. Blackbeard possessed a commanding presence that
instilled fear in those who encountered him. He exuded confidence and authority, which further enhanced his reputation as a
pirate leader and living up to his brand. Opponents would often

surrender as soon as Blackbeard hoisted the pirate flag bearing his brand, as they were terrorized by his appearance, reputation, and stories of the brutality of his attacks.

Blackbeard had a distinctive flag that he flew on his ships. The flag attributed to Blackbeard is commonly referred to as the Jolly Roger. However, it's important to note that there are no surviving examples of Blackbeard's actual flag, so the design we associate with him today is based on historical accounts and artistic depictions. The commonly recognized design for Blackbeard's flag features a white skull in the center, often depicted wearing a pirate's hat, with the skull placed on a black background. The flag also includes crossed bones beneath the skull, creating a menacing and intimidating image. The purpose of such flags was to strike fear into the hearts of Blackbeard's opponents and signify that they were dealing with pirates. Blackbeard's flag, like those of other pirates, was meant to be a warning to other ships. The flag was intended to intimidate and instill fear, making it clear that resistance against Blackbeard's crew would result in deadly consequences. Although the majority of Blackbeard's brand was built on brutally executed battles, he was not opposed to negotiating a peaceful surrender. There are many instances where a bloodless surrender was negotiated strictly based on the overwhelming fear of the Blackbeard brand.

Blackbeard's flag was his logo, and a logo is a critical part of an organization's brand. Blackbeard's skull and crossbones have become the Xerox of pirate flags as a universal symbol for pirates in general. Blackbeard's pirate logo of the skull and crossbones immediately conveys the message of death to anyone foolish enough to challenge the pirate. It is also one of the most globally recognized symbols for poisonous chemicals that is understood in any language or any country. The logo is often the first thing a potential customer will see, and it needs to instantly represent the desired message visually.

LESSONS IN ACTION

Starting a small business is hard. I woke up one morning in 2013 and realized, with great trepidation, that after forty-plus years in manufacturing leadership positions, I now found myself a small business owner. What follows is an account of my journey transitioning from a career of making stuff to having to sell myself and my services. When I woke up that day, I thought, "I have a company, I have services, but I have no customers. What now?" Coming from a family of entrepreneurs and sales professionals, I had direct access to a vast amount of experience to draw from. I was also fortunate to have a good colleague and friend in the business who provided and continues to provide invaluable advice, counsel, and guidance.

The first decision needed was the company name. This may seem like a no-brainer, but this was a struggle for me. Do I leverage my name recognition in the industry or create an autonomous name? After much discussion with family, friends, and colleagues plus market research, I ignored all the feedback and advice and named the company after myself. After a year, I rebranded the company with a name that reflected what the company does. Best decision ever. The lesson here is don't take this task lightly and focus on what you do, not who you are.

The second decision was the logo. The logo is just as important as the company name, as it is the first thing people see and one of the sticky things people remember. Just like the name, it should be a visual representation of what the company does. I would advise that you don't try to develop this yourself; the last thing you want to convey is a logo that was obviously self-developed and does not represent your brand appropriately. Hire a professional graphics/branding company to develop it for you.

A very painful lesson I learned is that the key to success is to laser focus on what you do. When I first launched the business, my list of services was extremely large and disconnected. When I rebranded the business, the company name, logo, and services were totally in sync and laser focused. The adage "you can't be all things to all people" is especially true in my case. Another painful lesson learned is that my likes and dislikes do not necessarily reflect what my customers like. Again, as with the logo, I would strongly suggest getting professional help from people whose job is to understand your market and how your product or services fit in.

Once your brand is created, it takes daily diligence to continuously build your brand. The biggest lesson to be learned here is that every single contact you have with a customer or potential customer is an opportunity to reinforce your brand. Your business card is a powerful tool that can make or break that first PO after an introduction. The mistake I made here was to cram my first business card with things that don't belong on a card, filling up both sides. That is the fastest way to get a potential customer to toss your card in the circular file instead of adding it to their contacts. I took a minimalist approach with the rebranded card that resulted in a simple, clean look with a blank back. Especially during large meetings and trade shows, people like to make notes on the back of business cards, and since the goal is to get someone to keep your card, this works.

In today's business environment, you are your brand. Defining your brand is the most important decision a business owner will make before any product or service is provided. Choose well, put in the work, and don't be afraid to bring in a professional to help get it right.

TAKEAWAYS

Park your ego. Understand that what appeals to you may not appeal to your target market. Solicit feedback on branding with a small group of people you trust from your target market, and listen.

Creating a logo is a process. It includes research, conceptualization, reflection, revisions, market research, and design. Make sure your logo clearly communicates what you do.

Make your brand "sticky." It needs to be memorable and enduring enough to remain relevant in 10, 20, … years. Be unique and clever, but avoid cutesy or trendy styles.

Focus on your message. Your brand must differentiate your business in a world of infinite choices. Don't expect instant success; it may take time for your brand to be recognized and associated with your business.

LESSON 10

MAKE PERCEPTION REALITY

"This Beard was black, which he suffered to grow of an extravagant Length; as to Breadth, it came up to his Eyes; he was accustomed to twist it with Ribbons, in small Tails, and turn them about his Ears: In Time of Action, he wore a sling over his Shoulders, with three Brace of Pistols, hanging in Holsters like Bandaliers; and stuck lighted Matches under his Hat, which appearing on each Side of his Face, his Eyes naturally looking fierce and wild, made him altogether such a Figure, that Imagination cannot form an Idea of a Fury, from Hell, to look more frightful."
–Charles Johnson on Blackbeard the Pirate

Effective leadership often involves motivating and maintaining the loyalty of the team. Blackbeard was known to be charismatic and capable of rallying his crew. His reputation as a fearsome and successful pirate played a major role in inspiring loyalty and obedience among his followers. As a pirate whose livelihood came from overpowering and capturing other ships, Blackbeard understood the importance of perception in his line of work. He was intentional in creating the image of Blackbeard and establishing his fearsome reputation. How did Blackbeard get his name?

According to popular legend, Blackbeard acquired his name

due to his intimidating appearance. He would tie slow-burning fuses into his beard and light them during battles, causing smoke to billow around his face. This gave him a fearsome and demonic appearance with his beard wreathed in smoke. The phrase "Your reputation precedes you" seems to have been coined specifically for Blackbeard. Tales of his exploits and the brutality of his battles spread far and wide, making sailing vessels think twice about traveling anywhere near his domain.

Blackbeard was a shrewd and calculating businessman who knew that intimidation and fear mattered greatly as a pirate. Often the battle was won before any swords were drawn as the mere mention of the name Blackbeard would strike fear in the hearts of his opponents. If they did not flat-out surrender, his fierce reputation of destroying his enemies was a debilitating weight in the back of their minds. Blackbeard intimidated his opponents with his fearsome, larger-than-life image because it was good business: if they gave up without a fight, he could keep their ship and fortune and not lose any men.

Blackbeard had a good grasp of human nature and was known for his effective use of psychological tactics to intimidate his enemies and enhance his reputation as a fearsome pirate. What follows are a few examples of the psychological tactics Blackbeard employed to transform the perception he wanted to be associated with him into reality in the eyes of his enemies as the most feared pirate of his time.

The Use of His Fearsome Appearance: Blackbeard cultivated a menacing image by wearing fuses or slow-burning matches in his beard, which he would light before entering battle. This created an aura of smoke and gave him an even more fearsome and demonic appearance. Adding to this terrifying image, Blackbeard strapped multiple pistols to his chest, along with knives and his sword. It is said that he deliberately used these tactics to strike fear into the hearts of his opponents.

Intimidating Displays: Blackbeard would often tie slow matches or fuses to his hat and light them during battles. This created an eerie atmosphere, with smoke billowing around his face, further enhancing his intimidating presence. The sight of him with smoke and fire emanating from his body would have undoubtedly struck fear into the hearts of his adversaries.

Exaggerating His Reputation: Blackbeard actively promoted his reputation as a ferocious and ruthless pirate. He often braided his beard with ribbons and tied them with small trinkets or colored pieces of string. This theatrical display was meant to draw attention to his appearance and assert his dominance.

Strategic Timing: Blackbeard was known to carefully time his attacks and raids to maximize their psychological impact. He would often strike at dawn or dusk when visibility was limited, creating a sense of uncertainty and chaos among his targets. This tactic added to the element of surprise and further disoriented his opponents.

Spreading Rumors: Blackbeard and his crew were not shy about spreading exaggerated tales of their exploits. These stories often portrayed them as merciless and bloodthirsty, further fueling their fearsome reputation. The mere mention of Blackbeard's name was sometimes enough to intimidate potential targets into surrendering without a fight.

It's worth noting that while Blackbeard's psychological tactics were undoubtedly effective, there are also elements of legend and myth surrounding his persona. Some accounts of his deeds may have been embellished or distorted over time. Nevertheless, his reputation as a fearsome and formidable pirate endures in popular culture.

LESSONS IN ACTION

Blackbeard understood that he wanted a single association when people thought of him: fear. A brand is simply the associations that exist in the minds of customers when they think about you and/or your company. Consider the message, emotions, and call to action you want your brand to elicit. If it doesn't address all three of these, go back to the drawing board. Successful branding is a competitive advantage; your brand should instantly connect the customer to the core purpose of your business. How many times have you talked to a friend about a great new commercial but struggled to identify the commercial with a particular product or company? A good brand makes this connection every time regardless of how good or distracting the marketing message is. Branding matters.

"Perception is reality." I used to have this quote hanging in my office to constantly remind me of this fact. Perception is particularly important in the context of leadership, as people are constantly watching, evaluating, and judging leaders by their actions, attitudes, and how they relate to others. How many times do we see a company promoting themselves as being a "world-class" manufacturer of widgets or as having been voted "best-in-class" at customer service? Who voted? This common issue is a perfect example of the truth in advertising dilemma. What often happens is a Dilbert cartoon in the making; a group of senior managers get together and declare, "You know, we do a pretty respectable job in our business, our quality is good, and our customers are mostly happy, let's begin selling ourselves as world-class." There is complete agreement and everyone pats themselves on the back for this brilliant decision. It then gets put on the website and marketing literature and they are off and running.

What does it mean to be world-class? Breaking it down into a single bullet point means being on par with the top performers in your chosen craft. Of course, numerous quantitative metrics are used to measure this, such as turnover, quality certifications, productivity, and the requisite financial ratios. But perhaps the most important metric is qualitative. How do your customers think you are doing? I have sat in on many management meetings where customer satisfaction is reported, discussed, and actioned. Quality and on-time delivery (OTD) are two universal measurements of customer satisfaction with most companies. It is always eye-opening for the management team when the internal metrics are put up for discussion, followed by customer scorecards.

Invariably, there is a significant disconnect between the two data sets with the internal numbers reflecting a better rating than the customers. This gap in perception needs to be addressed to align the internal measurements with the customer's. It could be that the customer's data is not accurate; many are famously bad at adjusting delivery dates in their system to reflect changes made by the customer. If a company is not diligent in validating customer ratings notifying them of inaccuracies, the system will still spit out supplier ratings that reflect these inaccuracies. While unfair, the customer doesn't know their data is not correct if you don't tell them. Perception is reality, but you can manage how others see your product, service, and reputation.

TAKEAWAYS

Manage perceptions. Perception is reality; first impressions count and are often irreversible. It may take years of exemplary performance to overcome a poor first impression.

Be authentic. The level of authenticity is key to perception and your customers can tell when you are not. Trust is earned from being true to oneself, genuine, and sincere.

Define your hook. Identify why a customer should buy *your* product over the competition. Include a tagline that tells your story and embodies your product and core values.

Learn from your kids. Notice what brands they embrace and what makes them indelible in your kid's minds. The fundamentals are the same whether you are selling cereal or sophisticated electronics.

CATHERINE THE GREAT

ON KEYS TO SUCCESS
1729-1796

As the empress of Russia, Catherine the Great is a bit of a contradiction in terms, as her name was not Catherine, nor was she Russian. Born Sophie Friederike Auguste on May 2, 1729, she began life as a minor German princess, growing up with a father famous for his military leadership and a mother who had little interest in her. As a teenager, her family moved to Russia, where Sophie converted to the Russian Orthodox faith and received a new name, Yekaterina or Catherine. Catherine knew what she wanted in life from an early age, and as a teen of great beauty, and prodded by her aunt, she began sending letters and pictures of herself to the grandson of Peter the Great, heir to the throne. Through time Catherine was able to orchestrate this relationship into a political union that ended with her marriage to young Peter III. Although strictly political, the marriage was doomed from the start, as Catherine was a strong young woman of prodigious intellect while Peter was a child in a man's body.

With no motive other than gaining power, she married into the royal family as a grand duchess. When the current Russian

Empress Elizabeth died in January 1762 and Peter ascended to the throne, Russia was engaged in the Seven Years' War against Prussia. Peter, now emperor, pulled Russia out of the war and allied with Frederick II of Prussia. For reasons not entirely known, Peter made plans to rid himself of his wife, but by that time Catherine had gained the support of the public and, more importantly, the army, and was alerted of the plan. On June 28, 1762, with the aid of her current lover, Grigory Orlov, Catherine had her husband arrested, demanding that Peter abdicate the throne. She then declared herself Catherine II, the sole ruler of Russia. Eight days after Peter III stepped down, Catherine ordered his execution.

Catherine's reign was not without controversy and criticism. Her policies toward serfdom, which maintained the institution rather than abolishing it, have been a subject of debate among historians. Additionally, her personal life and relationships, including alleged affairs and political intrigues, have added to her intriguing legacy. During her decades of tyrannical rule, Catherine expanded Russian control by first shrewdly installing her many lovers to positions of power in other countries. As leader, Catherine ruled with absolute power and expanded the country's borders through military might and diplomatic prowess. The high cost of her military campaigns combined with her oppressive social system provoked a major peasant uprising in 1773 after Catherine legalized the selling of serfs separate from the land. During her thirty-four-year rule, the longest of any woman in Russian history, she launched many wars, including the war against the Ottomans in 1768. After six years of brutal fighting and significant loss of life, the Ottomans ceded the Russian territories along the northern coast of the Black Sea and the Balkans. Catherine then tried to extend Russia's power west and launched attacks against Poland after joining forces with Prussia and Austria. A supreme military strategist, Catherine was just as shrewd in her political aspirations as in her war campaigns, leaving a trail of deceit, conquests, and bodies in her wake. Despite numerous historical rumors of more colorful circumstances, Catherine the Great died quietly in her bed on November 17, 1796, at the age of sixty-seven after suffering a stroke.

Catherine's reign was thirty-eight years long, the longest of any woman ruler, and was exceptionally successful and the lasting impact of her rule was undeniable. Catherine lived an extraordinary life and was able to avoid the pitfalls of a job that often ended in a bloody coup and terrible rebellions. Catherine the Great's leadership story is one of ambition, intellectual curiosity, and strategic decision-making. She left a lasting impact on Russia, modernizing the country, expanding its territory, and positioning it as a major player on the European stage. Her legacy as an enlightened despot continues to be debated, but there is no doubt that she was a formidable and influential ruler.

LESSON 11

FOCUS ON WHAT
YOU CONTROL

"Don't worry about things you cannot alter."
–Catherine the Great

Catherine the Great saw little value in endless planning for events that may never happen. Instead, she remained laser focused on what she had influence over and planned to maximize those results. She employed various strategies during her reign as Empress of Russia on activities that would expand her power, modernize the country, and pursue her ambitious goals. Here are some of the key strategies she utilized to make things happen:

Catherine understood the importance of diplomatic relations and alliances to protect Russian interests and secure her position as a European power. She engaged in diplomatic negotiations and formed alliances with other European nations, particularly against the Ottoman Empire. These alliances provided support during wars and helped maintain a balance of power.

Catherine pursued a policy of military expansion to increase the territory and influence of the Russian Empire. She waged wars and military campaigns, such as the Russo-Turkish War, the partitions of Poland, and the annexation of Crimea, to acquire new territories and expand Russian control. Military conquests allowed her to strengthen the empire and extend its reach.

Catherine recognized the importance of public perception and utilized cultural propaganda as a tool for promoting her image and the prestige of the Russian Empire. She cultivated relationships with intellectuals, writers, and artists, supporting their work and promoting the idea of Russia as a hub of culture and enlightenment. This cultural patronage helped shape a positive image of her reign and the empire itself.

Catherine used strategic marriages to strengthen alliances, secure foreign support, and solidify her position. She married into the Romanov dynasty, gaining legitimacy as the rightful heir to the throne. Additionally, she arranged marriages for her children and grandchildren with prominent European families to create political alliances and forge connections with other powerful nations.

Enlightenment was an intellectual movement in Europe during the seventeenth and eighteenth centuries that broke away from the Catholic Church as the country's undisputed religious and intellectual leader. Secularism, which was based on facts and reason, reshaped the way people saw issues like liberty, individual rights, and equality. Catherine embraced Enlightenment ideals and positioned herself as an enlightened monarch. She corresponded with Enlightenment thinkers, such as Voltaire, and expressed support for their ideas. However, she also selectively applied these ideals to further her political agenda and maintain her absolute power, using Enlightenment concepts to justify her rule and reforms.

These strategies allowed Catherine the Great to consolidate her power, expand the Russian Empire, and pursue her vision of a modernized Russia. Her diplomatic acumen, military prowess, cultural patronage, and manipulation of Enlightenment ideals contributed to her success as one of Russia's most influential and long-ruling monarchs.

LESSONS IN ACTION

A fly on the wall in conference rooms around corporate America would reveal that executives spend far too much time planning for things outside of their control and far too little time planning for things they can. The key concept Catherine the Great was talking about was not wasting energy and resources on endless "what ifs" that she had absolutely no control over. Her strategy was to instead put all of her resources toward maximizing the things she could control and positioning her armies to be able to react to any uncontrollable issues when and if they occurred. This is a sound strategy for a leader in any business situation and one that has proved especially effective in times of uncertainty. To illustrate with a sports analogy, a golfer can't control how fast the greens are or how his opponent plays any more than a business executive can control the stock market or his competition's business plan. What the golfer can control is how she adjusts to the green speed and how well she is playing.

One company I worked at in my younger years would have weekly one-hour leadership meetings with the senior managers of the company, chaired by the owner. Staff meetings are an important aspect of effective communication and coordination within an organization. They provide an opportunity for team members to come together, share information, discuss important topics, and collaborate on projects. This meeting should have been a productive setting for each department head to report on any internal issues they were having, review feedback from customers, and plan the day-to-day operational activities required to run a business. What happened instead was forty-five minutes of the owner fretting over what might happen with the economy and discussing how ups and downs would impact employee head count, profits, and growth. Endless hours were spent devising plans for multiple "what ifs" that may never happen. This left fifteen minutes to discuss the things impactful to the business, many of which did need a plan to address real issues. Focusing on what you can control does not mean ignoring or neglecting the things outside your control. It's about acknowledging the limits of your influence and directing your attention and efforts toward areas where you can make a meaningful impact.

Worrying about uncontrollable conditions is counterproductive; there are plenty of things we can complain about, but it's a waste of emotional energy to focus on things we cannot control. The ultimate test for us as leaders is to focus on the controllables. And while contingency plans for things like economic swings and competitive pressures will always be a part of strategic planning, concentrating on your needle movers is always money better spent.

TAKEAWAYS

Mind what matters. Master what you can control, fatigue and burnout is less related to the actual work you do than to worry and frustration.

Lower your anxiety level. If you are overly worried about something outside of your control; write it down on a piece of paper and put it in a desk drawer and leave it there.

Block out the noise. Create and work off a priority list to stay focused and remove uncertainty and external influences from your thought process.

Don't worry, be happy. Statistics on what people worry about show that 40 percent never happen, 30 percent has already happened, 22 percent are needless or petty, and 8 percent actually happens. Of this, only 4 percent are within some level of our control.

LESSON 12

WORK HARD

"One does not always do the best there is.
One does the best one can."
– Catherine the Great

From the minute Catherine (then Sophie) arrived in Russia, she knew she wanted to become the Russian empress, perhaps influenced by her highly opportunistic mother, Johanna. Catherine worked extremely hard and everything she did from that point on was done in pursuit of this desire. Before she rose to power, she took several steps as a young woman to position herself for this role. She first committed herself to learning Russian and could often be seen pacing the floor, reciting Russian until she became fluent. Catherine also knew that her pedigree as a princess of minor nobility would prohibit advancement to the level of ruler, so she took another strategic step. She married into the royal family by orchestrating a political marriage to the heir to the throne, Peter III, grandson of Peter the Great. The marriage elevated Catherine to the title of grand duchess. Catherine was a workaholic who was known for her industrious nature and dedication to improving her country. What follows are only a few examples of Catherine the Great working hard.

Catherine implemented numerous reforms aimed at modernizing Russia. She focused on improving the country's education system, healthcare, infrastructure, and agriculture. She invited foreign experts and scholars to Russia to contribute their knowledge and expertise.

Catherine engaged in extensive military campaigns to expand the Russian Empire. She fought against the Ottoman Empire and successfully annexed Crimea, greatly expanding Russia's territory and influence.

Catherine worked on several legislative reforms to strengthen the rule of law and promote justice. She drafted a new legal code known as the Nakaz, which aimed to modernize and streamline Russia's legal system.

Catherine was a great patron of the arts and sciences and established the Hermitage Museum in Saint Petersburg, which houses an extensive collection of art and cultural artifacts. Catherine also supported the works of prominent writers, philosophers, and intellectuals of her time.

Catherine engaged in extensive correspondence with philosophers and thinkers of the Enlightenment era, including Voltaire and Denis Diderot. She actively sought their counsel, demonstrating her commitment to intellectual pursuits and the exchange of knowledge.

Catherine was known for her rigorous work ethic and hands-on approach to governance. She spent countless hours reviewing reports, making decisions, and personally overseeing various administrative matters. She was known to work late into the night and was often seen as an example of diligence and dedication.

Catherine played a crucial role in Russian foreign policy. She skillfully navigated complex diplomatic relationships, negotiated treaties, and formed alliances to protect Russia's interests and maintain its position as a major European power.

These examples illustrate Catherine the Great's tireless efforts to transform Russia into a modern and influential nation as well as her dedication to intellectual and cultural advancement.

LESSONS IN ACTION

I believe the foundation of leadership is formed by a person's work ethic, their belief in the moral benefit and importance of work and its inherent ability to strengthen character. The traits of a strong work ethic are the very same traits of a strong leader: professionalism, respectfulness, dependability, dedication, determination, accountability, and humility. A great leader embodies each of these traits and encourages others to embrace them as part of the continual development process.

Being a lifelong Midwesterner, I can attest to the "Midwest work ethic" being a real thing. It refers to the cultural values and attitudes toward work that are often associated with the Midwestern region of the United States. While generalizations about an entire region can be oversimplified, the Midwest is known for its strong work ethic and emphasis on hard work, self-discipline, and dedication to one's job. Additionally, the Midwest is often associated with traditional values and a no-nonsense approach to work. People from the region are known for their practicality, down-to-earth attitudes, and focus on productivity. The emphasis on humility and modesty also plays a role as Midwesterners tend to value hard work as a means to achieve success rather than seeking recognition or attention for their efforts.

I am so very lucky to have had such positive role models in my parents, which is how the foundation of my work ethic was formed at an early age. Our family owned a printed circuit board manufacturing company, and before I was old enough to work there full time, I would spend afternoons after school taking out garbage and cleaning toilets. Remember the humility trait? Well, nothing is more humbling and character building than cleaning toilets every afternoon. I didn't know it then, but this experience would resonate with me years later as I moved into my first leadership role. Of course, the employees remember my early years at the company and I believe it earned me some respect as the boss that wasn't too important to clean toilets. Working in the business would become my first full-time job after escaping high school and the beginning of my leadership career. This is where I learned my first leadership lesson. What I have found is that people in this position, children of business owners, have two paths they can take.

The first path is to embrace the privileged role of being the owner's kid and all of the perks that come along with that. Everyone has probably experienced a scenario in which the owner's kid feels that they don't have to work hard and that the grunt work is below them. The second path, the one I chose, is to work harder than everyone else to lead by example so that there was no doubt which path I had chosen. The collateral benefit from this work ethic is the respect that gets earned. I also believe that great leadership comes from having been there and done the work.

TAKEAWAYS

Outwork everyone. There is a direct correlation between hard work and success. The old adage that "The harder you work, the luckier you get" is true; laziness inspires no one.

Choose a path. Working hard is contagious, and unfortunately, the opposite is also true. Be the leader that inspires others to choose the right path by the example you set.

Do the grunt work. Nothing motivates others more than a leader that gets their hands dirty working side by side with them.

Work hard, play hard. It is important to recognize that there must be a work/life balance and that success requires both hard work and the ability to unwind and enjoy life.

NAPOLEON BONAPARTE

ON VISIONARY LEADERSHIP
1769 – 1829

Born on the island of Corsica in 1769, Napoleon Bonaparte was a French military leader and emperor who conquered much of Europe in the early nineteenth century. One of eight surviving children (his mother gave birth to twelve), Napoleon's childhood was challenging. Although the family was from minor nobility, they were not wealthy and his father was not a regular presence in his life. His father's death at the age of thirty-eight left the family destitute, but his mother would become a major influence who would instill the moral compass and passion that would form the foundation for his later success. A curious child, he showed an early aptitude for learning and was sent to the military school in Brienne at the age of ten where he excelled in math, history, and literature. After graduating, Bonaparte continued to develop his intellectual and military skills at the elite military academy in Paris and became an artillery officer after graduation. Stationed in the south of France, the young officer worked in the trenches to learn the practical side of war, weaponry, and tactics. All of these early experiences had a strong impact on his personality and leadership style, leading to his extraordinary military success.

The French Revolution began in 1789 and was the result of the attempt to raise taxes by King Louis XVI. Already pushed to their limits by the king's oppressive rule and the poor conditions of their lives, the people stormed the Bastille in protest and the revolution was born. Bonaparte rose quickly through the ranks of the military during the French Revolution and crowned himself the first emperor of France in 1804 after forcibly seizing political power in a 1799 coup. A brilliant tactician, Napoleon Bonaparte was a masterful soldier and a superb administrator. He was also a supreme narcissist and one of the cruelest dictators in history. After ten years of violence, civil unrest, and economic instability, Bonaparte is credited with ending the French Revolution. What distinguished Bonaparte from his contemporaries were his brilliant tactical plans that allowed him to win numerous battles against enemies that greatly outnumbered his troops. Due to this, Napoleon Bonaparte is often regarded as the greatest military commander in history.

Of historical note, during Napoleon's military campaign in Egypt, the Rosetta Stone was discovered, which provided the key to cracking the code of Egyptian hieroglyphics, a written language that had been dead for almost 2,000 years.

Bonaparte was exiled twice to remote islands after military defeats. The second was to the island of Saint Helena after the crushing loss in the Battle of Waterloo, where he soon died alone at the age of fifty-one in 1829. An autopsy determined that the cause of his death was stomach cancer (as was his father's), which has led to widespread speculation that long-term stomach pain was the reason Napoleon was often depicted with his hand in his vest. Interestingly, Napoleon has always been seen as a very short man (think Napoleon Complex), but at 5 feet, six inches, he was actually a couple of inches taller than the average height of French males at the time. Napoleon Bonaparte was a world game changer; he created a new form of government, implemented social and political reforms, and showed the world that revolution could overthrow a tyrannical government.

LESSON 13

CULTIVATE BUY-IN TO YOUR VISION

"A leader is a dealer in hope."
– Napoleon Bonaparte

Napoleon Bonaparte was steadfast in his vision, facilitation of a free and united Europe unrestrained by monarchy, throughout his career. In the aftermath of the French Revolution, people were desperately looking for a leader who could give them hope and lead them out of the chaos left behind. Bonaparte had a clear purpose and vision that was exactly what the masses were looking for and he quickly embraced the notion that he would become Europe's savior. Bonaparte famously said that a leader is a dealer in hope, and hope is what he offered. Hope does not imply blind faith, rather it comes with a sense of expectations, and Bonaparte had a clear vision that aligned with the problem the people wanted solved, post-revolution anarchy. In 1795, a new government and constitution were established to protect France's newfound freedom. After being torn apart by a civil war between the royalists and revolutionaries, people wanted and needed law and order. The new government's mission was to create a system of government that broke away from the oppression of the entitled, privileged monarchy that had ruled for years. Unfortunately, the new government proved weak and incapable of accomplishing the mission. The government was bankrupt and unemployment, inflation, and taxes were spiraling, and the government had lost control of the country. This is where Napoleon Bonaparte came in.

A few members of the new government secretly approached Bonaparte with the sentiment that he was the only man who could save France, which was music to his ears. Bringing in several loyal officers, they began planning their coup to bring down the current government. The coup d'état was set for November 9, 1799, and through military force and a winning strategy, the coup took only two days. This essentially marked the end of the French Revolution and a vote was called for. On December 13, the new constitution was installed and a three-consul government was established. Bonaparte was named as first consul with full executive powers. A short five years later, Napoleon Bonaparte would become the emperor of France.

LESSONS IN ACTION

Anyone who has led an implementation of any new project understands the challenge of getting people to buy-in to the change. The natural human tendency is to resist change because it represents the unknown. The current state is comfortable and does not require a lot of thought, it's just part of the norm. To get true buy-in people need to believe in the leader to believe in the vision. As we look at the reasons why people don't buy-in to a leader's vision there are ample examples in our work and personal lives: politics, church, marriage (the list is endless). It doesn't matter how strong the vision is, the leader can't be successful if they can't move others to action or change, in other words, buy-in. There are two paths these things can take, and let's use implementing a new business management system for illustrative purposes:

Path 1: A small steering committee is established that is comprised entirely of management. Over a considerable amount of time, the committee creates all the new business processes in a silo with the only constructive discussion being among themselves. This re-engineering of the system includes processes, standard work, procedures, work instructions, forms, and checklists. Once the committee is satisfied with the new system, they proudly roll it out by telling the workforce, "This is the new way of doing your job."

Path 2. A small group is created for each process comprised of the subject matter experts, the people who are actually doing the day-to-day work. The leader of the entire project gives each group a thorough understanding of why this change is needed and presents the requirements that need to be met. The group is then told, "Here is what we need to accomplish with this re-engineering, your task is to find a way to get there." The groups are given complete autonomy to develop their processes and encouraged to challenge any current norms. Once each process is complete, the group presents its solutions to the leadership team for feedback and concurrence.

Which do you think has the highest success rate? (rhetorical question) Path 1 is being forced down the throats of the employees while in Path 2 the employees have skin in the game. Anytime the people doing the job are actively engaged in the change, buy-in is assured and they become cheerleaders for the change. Win-Win. The following is a case study I did for a client who had a bad experience with implementing lean manufacturing in one of their divisions. This illustrates the peril of following Path 1.

CASE STUDY: COMPANY A

Company A has 1,500 employees and manufactures high-volume, low-cost widgets in a very competitive global marketplace.

The prior year's profits were marginal but positive at $4.5 million on $145 million in revenue (3.3 percent). The widget manufacturer was just acquired by a very large company in an unrelated industry, which was unimpressed with the new division's performance. Having had great success implementing a lean program, the parent company suggests that Company A investigate implementing lean to improve the division's performance. Company A hires a team of lean consultants over nine months to come in and "do lean for them." The below data represents the five-year profit results after the implementation of Company A's lean program.

Year 0: $4.5MM (baseline)

Year 1: $5.5MM

Year 2: $5.6MM

Year 3: $4.3MM

Year 4: $4.1MM

Year 5: $3.9MM

POSTMORTEM

So what went wrong? Quite simply, the consultants left! Of course, they had done exactly what they were hired to do; they did lean for Company A. The consulting team had come in and retooled all the procedures and methodologies, and the program rollout created enough momentum to sustain itself for a few years. Some training had taken place, but the workforce had no real understanding of why things had been changed or any concept of value versus non-value activities. The passage of time, combined with employee and management turnover, resulted in things gradually falling back to the way they used to be. In fact, due to the confusion created by all the changes by the consultants, profits began to slip below the pre-lean baseline beginning in year three post-lean implementation. Old habits truly do die hard! By the way, in June of year six after lean implementation, Company A was closed down by the parent company for underperformance. Had Company A followed Path 2 instead, the results would be very different and they would still be in business.

Buy-in is all about the leader. Many people have it backward, which is the fundamental reason they fail. They believe that if the cause is good enough, people will automatically buy-in and follow. But it doesn't work that way. People don't follow worthy causes; they follow worthy leaders. People buy-in to the leader first, then the leader's vision.

TAKEAWAYS

Become a leader people want to follow. Look in the mirror with a critical eye and determine if you are a leader that you would follow.

Engage the stakeholders. People have a sense of ownership when they are part of the solution. Pride in ownership fosters buy-in and pride is contagious.

Exhibit passion for your vision. People watch the behaviors of their leaders very closely and your level of passion will influence their willingness to buy-in.

Address a need. People are more willing to support a change that directly impacts them in a positive way.

LESSON 14

ADJUST TO THE SITUATION

Napoleon Bonaparte was one of the more successful wartime planners before the twentieth century and most certainly of his time. He was often seen by candlelight in his window as he worked through the nights leading up to a campaign. This time was spent planning his offense, defense, and countermeasures to any actions his opponent might employ. It was said that Napoleon was brilliant at anticipating the movements and strategy of the enemy, but that brilliance was born out of his obsession with planning. Every point/counterpoint was defined and analyzed for the impact on the outcome of the conflict and every contingency accounted for. In essence, Bonaparte was a master project manager; he assembled a strategic planning cabinet that would conduct research on the opponent's past strategies and results as well as anticipate potential risks with his plan. The cabinet also coordinated communication between the tactical commanders and kept everyone informed and on the same page regarding the status and any changes to the plan.

This proved to be an extremely effective planning strategy that resulted in unprecedented success in his battles. Napoleon was also flexible in his thinking and was not afraid to change and adapt his plan based on the counsel of his cabinet.

Bonaparte's planning expertise and flexibility were never more evident than during the Ulm Campaign. In 1805, Bonaparte was planning on crossing the English Channel to invade Great Britain with 2,000 ships and 200,000 soldiers. France and Britain were at odds again over who would rule the European continent and Napoleon was determined to decide this himself. As his soldiers prepared to cross the Channel, Bonaparte suddenly ordered them to retreat from England and move into Europe, to the surprise of everyone. He had learned that Austria and Russia had joined forces to destroy him, and he needed a new plan. His intelligence told him that waiting for them were two massive armies that outnumbered Bonaparte's French army two to one and that the Austrian and Russian strategy was to defeat his army through sheer force.

While analyzing this new information, Napoleon quickly recognized the flaw in the allies' plans; the Austrian forces were spread out across the continent, which negated their overwhelming numbers advantage. He believed that if he moved fast enough, he could isolate and defeat the Austrian army before the Russians had a chance to join them. And he did, marching his 200,000 men 500 miles in only forty days. They were able to surprise and surround General Karl Mack and the Austrian army, forcing a surrender of over 27,000 men without a single casualty. This was only one of many military and political victories that added to the prestige and popularity of Napoleon Bonaparte.

LESSONS IN ACTION

The best leaders are those who have mastered "situational leadership," in other words, adjusting their leadership style to best fit the current situation. A leader must read a situation and instinctively know what play to call. Unfortunately, intuition cannot be learned; what you are born with is all you get. However, you can learn to be more aware of the constraints and factors impacting a situation, and experience will teach lessons learned to improve your decisions going forward. The ability to adjust and pivot your leadership style to address changing circumstances is a core trait that all great leaders possess, and Napoleon Bonaparte was a master.

Having a working knowledge of human nature, behavior, and psychology can make a difference when assessing a current situation and determining the need to change course. The leadership style that would be most successful with a group of engineers is far different from the style required to lead a group of soldiers. The former requires a collaborative approach that gives the engineers a sense of autonomy, while with the latter, an autocratic approach is needed with life-or-death situations such as military operations and law enforcement. Each leadership style is equally effective in its specific circumstances, but would be disastrous if the styles were reversed.

A perfect example of an incredibly successful situational leader is former NBA coach Phil Jackson. Phil Jackson is considered to be one of the greatest coaches in the history of the NBA. Jackson has one of the highest winning percentages of any Hall of Fame coach, eleven championships, and is the only coach to win at least double-digit championships in any major US professional sport. In the basketball world, Phil Jackson is often referred to as the "Zen Master," a contradiction to the typical hard-nosed, autocratic approach of a majority of other coaches. His unique coaching practices integrated meditation, Buddhism, and other spiritual traditions.

I lived in Chicago during the Michael Jordan years and was obsessed with Jordan's Bulls, not missing a single game on TV between 1986 and 1997. Case in point: I remember on one family vacation we planned to go to a well-known amusement park in that state. Much to my dismay, I found out that the day of the excursion happened to be on the same day as Game 3 of a Bulls NBA finals game. I immediately ran out to the local electronics store and purchased a battery-operated portable TV, which I lugged around the park so I could watch the game in between rides with the family. The Bulls won six championships (two three-peats) during this time and each three-peat team required a different leadership style from Jackson. Michael Jordan and Scottie Pippen were the only constant, and the team dynamics were very different, as the makeup of the supporting cast would change.

During the first seven years of Jordan's career, it was "The Michael Jordan Show" with Jordan scoring 40+ points a night as the team continued to lose. It was clear early on that Jordan was destined for greatness and Jackson's challenge was how to get the best player in the league to share the ball. The issue wasn't that Michael was selfish but that he didn't trust his teammates to make the shot. Jackson first presented a challenge to the team, saying that they had to earn Jordan's trust and if they wanted him to give them the ball, they needed to come through when he did.

Perhaps the defining moment in Jordan's growth came during Game 5 of the 1991 NBA Finals when Jackson finally convinced Jordan to trust his teammates. He did this by asking Jordan a question during a critical time in the game when the Bulls were in jeopardy of losing and facing a Game 6. He asked Michael to tell him who was open on the court when he got double-teamed. Jordan said Paxson (John Paxson) and Jackson simply said to pass him the ball. On the next possession, Jordan did just that and trusted Paxon to come through. His trust was rewarded as Paxson put on a scoring clinic with 10 points in a couple of minutes. This turned the game around and played a huge role in the team winning the first championship of Jordan's career.

The second three-peat team featured a rebellious, highly polarizing player named Dennis Rodman. An extremely dominant rebounder and defender, Rodman had worn out his welcome with numerous teams that would not put up with his antics. He was labeled "uncoachable," and Jackson knew that if he tried to control Rodman, he would fail just as the other coaches had. Part of Jackson's style was to bond with his players, and he knew that Rodman idolized Michael Jordan and would listen to Michael. Rodman required a lot of emotional maintenance and both Jordan and Jackson were constantly reinforcing that the team needed him and could not win a championship without him. This approach worked, with Rodman playing some of the best basketball of his career and the team winning another three championships.

I still remember as clearly as yesterday being in the car when the news came over the radio that the Bulls had just signed Rodman. I immediately called my brother and said, "Rodman is the missing piece, the Bulls are going to win another three-peat," and the rest, of course, is history.

TAKEAWAYS

Leading is like a chess match. It is no coincidence that the leaders most proficient at adapting to changing situations are also the most successful.

Plan for all contingencies. There is no such thing as being over prepared; have a Plan B, a Plan C, and a Plan D. Spend as much time anticipating contingencies as is spent on the original plan.

Execute, assess, and adjust. A good plan executed today is usually better than a great plan executed tomorrow. Good plans can become great plans after assessing the early results and adjusting.

Reject equality. The biggest mistake a leader can make is to treat everyone equally. Everyone has a unique personality that responds differently; a leader needs to account for this.

AL CAPONE

ON BUILDING A SUCCESSFUL ORGANIZATION
1899-1947

Born January 17, 1899, in Brooklyn, New York, Alphonsus Capone is perhaps America's most widely recognized gangster and the single greatest icon of the collapse of law and order in the United States during the 1920s prohibition era. He was the son of Italian immigrants and had a very difficult childhood. Although Capone was kicked out of the sixth grade, he was extremely intelligent and streetwise at an early age. With time on his hands, he joined several teenage gangs, which began his lifelong career in crime. He married his longtime girlfriend, Mae, in 1918 and had one child, Sonny. Capone was an infamous womanizer throughout his life, which remained unchanged after his marriage. He contracted an STD from a prostitute at a mob club where he was a bouncer, which would ultimately result in his death many years later. Capone became the family provider after his father died when he was twenty-one. Fiercely devoted to his mother, he continued to call her every day even after he became one of the most feared mobsters of the era. Not uncommon for mobsters of his time, Capone took great pains to separate work from home to protect his family and shield them from any repercussions of his criminal activity.

Capone became "boss" of the Chicago Outfit in 1925 when Johnny Torrio retired after being seriously wounded in an assassination attempt. Capone built a fearsome reputation as a ruthless leader who eliminated his competition while acquiring "racketeering rights" to several areas of Chicago. Capone's "rackets" were created by the enactment of the prohibition amendment and included illegal brewing, distilling, and distribution of beer and liquor. While Capone considered these "growth industries," he also developed interests in legitimate businesses and cultivated influence with (bribed) receptive public officials, labor unions, and employee associations.

While Al Capone ordered the deaths of hundreds of men, he allowed the thug to live who'd carved up his face and unwittingly labeled Capone "Scarface" for the rest of his life. As incongruous as this may seem, Capone's sense of honor and integrity drove this decision as he knew his actions had led to the altercation and that he was in the wrong. He understood that a dishonorable reputation was bad for business and, make no mistake, Al Capone was all about business.

He was best known for the brutal St. Valentine's Day Massacre on February 14, 1929, when seven members of the rival "Bugs" Moran mob were machine-gunned against a garage wall by Capone's henchmen posing as police. The authorities were never able to convict Capone on any of his bootlegging, prostitution, and murder crimes. He was finally arrested at the age of thirty-three by the FBI, following a seven-year run as the boss of the Chicago Outfit. He was eventually charged with twenty-two counts of tax evasion, found guilty on five counts, and sentenced to eleven years in federal prison. While imprisoned, Capone's health and mental capacity started to decline drastically and his wife, Mae, was able to get him released for medical reasons. However, when released in 1939, Capone was unable to assume his rightful place as gangland boss due to a debilitating brain disease derived from the untreated syphilis he contracted in his early years. In 1947, eight days after his forty-eighth birthday, the most feared gangster of his era died in his home with the mental capacity of a twelve-year-old child.

Al Capone was easily the most infamous gangster of his time and built the most powerful organization of the Roaring Twenties. Capone's strong leadership allowed him to rule over a group of tough, hardened criminals and transform his little street gang into a major corporation.

LESSON 15

KNOW WHAT YOUR CUSTOMERS WANT

"I am just a businessman, giving the people what they want.
Some call it bootlegging. Some call it racketeering.
I call it a business."
– Al Capone

Al Capone did not decide to get into the business of selling illegal alcohol because it was something he had always wanted to do. He recognized a market opportunity and exploited it. The prohibition movement, formed in the late 1800s, believed that alcohol was the root of all the nation's problems. The leaders of the movement were alarmed at the drinking behaviors of Americans and believed that if alcohol was illegal, America would become a sober nation within thirty years. In 1919, Congress passed the National Prohibition Act, the Eighteenth Amendment, and the states ratified it shortly after. The prohibition amendment (as it was commonly called) prohibited the "manufacture, sale, or transportation of intoxicating liquors" across the United States. Curiously, the amendment did not prohibit the consumption, private possession, or production for one's own consumption of alcohol. Since beer and liquor could be consumed but not produced, Al Capone recognized a golden opportunity to monopolize the illegal production and distribution of alcohol to consumers who could legally drink it but had no supply.

Capone's syndicate was already involved in prostitution, bribery, narcotics trafficking, robbery, and protection rackets, but prohibition created a captive customer base for Capone that would generate more profits than all his other illegal activities combined. At the peak of his career as a crime lord, the Capone organization was bringing in over $100,000 per year, which is equivalent to over $1 billion today. These customers were primarily illegal liquor dealers and speakeasies. Capone was able to double-dip as he owned over 6,000 speakeasies, so he made a profit on the alcohol and the establishments. It was fairly easy for Capone to identify what his new customers wanted: alcohol. To meet this tremendous demand, he took over the thousands of breweries and distilleries across the nation.

No matter how big his target market was, Al Capone would not have been successful in the business of selling illegal alcohol if his customers were not happy with his product and service. He understood that being successful in business is all about understanding what customers want. As simple as this sounds, it doesn't matter how great you think your product or service is; no one will buy it if they don't want or believe they need it. What a customer wants is very simple, they want the core product or service of your business to meet their needs and expectations.

LESSONS IN ACTION

During a recent visit to a manufacturing company, the discussion turned to up-and-coming technology and what this company's plans were. The general manager, an ex-naval commander, said to me, "Anticipating what future needs our customers will have has been the biggest challenge we face." When I asked what their process was for understanding this, the answer was, "We are very reactive; we develop new technologies, processes, or products only after a customer, or customers, express a need for it."

I asked the commander if he had ever heard of Tom Peters, he said no, and I then relayed a story that Peters told during a speaking engagement I happened to be attending. He was talking about interviewing the owner of a very large steel mill that excelled in delighting the customer. When asked what his secret recipe was, the owner responded, "We have discovered a very rare and complicated method to fully understand the needs of our customers: *we talk to them!*"

This story has always stuck with me, and I could see from the commander's face that it resonated with him as well. What is the secret of the very successful companies in Peters's books? The answer is painfully simple; they listen to their customers. As I have said many times before, you may, in fact, be a world-class organization, but if your customers don't perceive you that way, it doesn't matter. It's extremely easy for the leaders of a company to assume they're keeping their customers happy. The challenge is in the ability to transform organizational culture into one that is driven by its customers' true needs. No level of performance is sustainable without an occasional adjustment, and the appropriate adjustment in strategy can only be developed after measuring your customers' needs and perceptions. Customer satisfaction is like any other process, and as I am known to frequently say, you can't improve what you haven't measured.

While there is something to be said about not wanting to be on the technological "bleeding edge" and the financial risk that comes along with it, you do not want to neglect customer needs and jeopardize the value proposition your company presents. With apologies to Kevin Costner, the "If we build it, they will come" philosophy does not translate in the financially prohibitive and capital-intensive manufacturing industry. However, there are proactive methods to understand future requirements that will prevent science projects and focus on real customer needs.

TAKEAWAYS

Talk to your customers. Understand the problems your company's product or service is solving. This is not a one and done activity; customer needs change and this is an ongoing process.

Stand in your customer's shoes. Every aspect of a business starts and ends with the customer, focus on their world, not yours.

Deliver on promises, every time. A single broken promise is remembered long after the good will of promises met are forgotten.

Perception is reality. The biggest mistake you can make is to assume your customers are happy. The care & feeding of your customers should be a top priority.

LESSON 16

STREAMLINE YOUR BUSINESS

"Capitalism. This American system of ours, call it Americanism, call it capitalism, call it what you will, gives every one of us a great opportunity if we only seize it with both hands and make the most of it."
– Al Capone

Al Capone might not have been your typical entrepreneur, considering he was actively involved in the illegal activities of bootlegging, bribery, prostitution, and smuggling. Just because Capone's businesses tended to run on the opposite side of the law doesn't mean he didn't know how to run a successful operation. Capone owned more than 300 businesses, many of which were legitimate. He commanded respect, got things done, and had the respect and loyalty of his employees, all traits in anyone's definition of a leader. While his methods were certainly barbaric in the classic business sense, his results were astounding. Al Capone's businesses bought in an astounding $20 million a week (in today's dollars!). When Al Capone took over the gang, the business grew exponentially and profits skyrocketed. As the business grew, Capone's criminal enterprise became known as "The Chicago Outfit," a name that wouldn't suggest a criminal enterprise if you didn't know what the true purpose of the business was. In many ways, Capone built his business much like a traditional organization. A typical day for him was spent in an office building, answering calls like the CEO of a traditional company. Capone's business model was relatively simple, with only three prongs:

1. Coordinate the importation of alcohol from other states and Canada.

2. Take over the thousands of breweries and distilleries nationwide.

3. Set up a supply chain system that includes truck drivers, salespeople, speakeasies (bars), and a heavily armed security force to protect the investments.

Capone soon dominated the bootlegging industry through persistence, hard work, and violent tactics. He created a syndicate of rival bootleggers, unheard of at the time, by convincing them it was good business to join and divide the distribution to minimize risks. This agreement also avoided violence between the groups and allowed everyone to still make money. He grew his bar business with a very effective tactic; he would tell the owners if they didn't buy beer from him, he would blow up their bar. Then he would pay to fix it, putting them in debt to Capone, which forced them to buy his beer. There also was an extreme element of fear in Capone's leadership. Everyone knew not to mess with Al Capone because those that did tended to disappear. He would kill anyone who tried to hurt any of his men or would kill any of his men who betrayed him. Capone would often brag to colleagues that he had about half of the Chicago police on his payroll, which fed his perception that he was untouchable. He would also rig elections to ensure that candidates he could control were elected. These are some of the strategies Capone would use to secure new business and grow existing revenue streams. He was extremely loyal, believing loyalty to be a critical trait in any business, but especially in his. Al Capone led with an iron fist and a smart strategy.

LESSONS IN ACTION

I spent twenty-three years in leadership positions in manufacturing companies before going to work for one of my largest customers. This company was growing quickly and was looking to find a person to fill a new leadership position to support this growth. I was charged with putting together a sourcing team of commodity specialists to develop and manage a new global supply base that could scale with the company's growing global footprint. In the fifteen years I was in this position, I got to work intimately with over 1,000 of the best manufacturing companies in the world and saw firsthand world-class business practices, technology, and efficiency. I also got to see the impact of poor business processes with companies that didn't make the grade. This presented an opportunity as it was clear that while many companies excelled in their respective fields, many did not and could benefit from my skill set and experience. That's when I started my consulting business, The Right Approach Consulting, with the mission of helping these types of companies improve and simplify their business processes. While my solutions are customized to each client's business and needs, there is a process I follow when engaging with a new client.

Step 1: Set expectations. While sitting down with the leadership team, I am typically asked immediately how I can help them. I tell them that before we discuss this, I first need to understand what their pain points are and what results they are looking for. Here I do a lot of listening and the client does a lot of talking. Then I explain that my goal is to make sure their processes work for the company and not the other way around. The definition of success is to simplify their business processes while improving organizational performance.

Step 2: Discovery. Once the expectations are set and agreed to, the next activity is to meet with each process owner and perform a comprehensive review of the current state of the particular process. Then we test every single activity that is being performed against the following three questions:

1.   Is it providing the results you want?

2.   Does it add value to the organization?

3.   How can it be simplified and improved?

Usually, the process is not working well or I wouldn't be there in the first place. Anything that is not adding value must be eliminated or re-engineered so that it does add value. Streamlining and improving the process will normally require exercising several improvement tools with a larger group of stakeholders. Then it is a matter of wash and repeat with every other process.

Step 3: Implementation and Training. A business process transformation like this requires training in the new or re-engineered processes, methods, and responsibilities. This is a complete organizational activity, from the leadership team down to the operator level. The process owners have skin in the game since they were involved in crafting the upgraded processes, so buy-in is strong during implementation. By focusing the project on satisfying those three questions throughout the organization, the results can be spectacular.

These three steps to simplify, streamline, and improve can be applied to manufacturing or service organizations in any business or market. Historical results for my clients average from 60 percent to 80 percent improvement in operational performance in reduced tasks, and lead times along with increases in efficiency, quality, and value-add activities.

TAKEAWAYS

Eliminate non-value-add activities. Nothing kills improvement faster than doing things that add no value to the company. Eliminating this "waste" will free up resources to work on what really matters.

Get stakeholder buy-in. Actively engaging the people that actually do the work in the re-engineering will minimize resistance and maximize results.

Question everything. Use a critical eye and accept nothing at face value. Things that are working well need to be challenged as much as things that aren't.

Understand simple is harder. The path of least resistance is to keep things the same. It requires a lot of work to reduce a complex process to a simple one and still maintain the integrity of it.

SONNY BARGER

ON EXTREME LEADERSHIP
1938-2022

For over fifty years, Ralph Hubert "Sonny" Barger presided over one of the most violent, and successful, operations in organized crime history, the Hells Angels Motorcycle Club (HAMC). Born October 8, 1938, Barger's mother left him with his alcoholic father and older sister when he was just four months old. His violent tendencies surfaced early with several school suspensions for assaulting teachers and fighting with his classmates. In 1955, he enlisted in the army at age sixteen and was discharged fourteen months later when it was discovered that he had forged his birth certificate to be able to join. After returning from the army, Barger, pronounced bar-grrr, rode with some small local motorcycle clubs but quickly left, disappointed in the lack of "brotherhood" and courage in the membership, two attributes that would become guiding principles of the Hells Angels. He began riding with some friends who shared his vision, and one of the bikers, Boots Don Reeves, wore a patch he had found in Sacramento of a small skull wearing an aviator cap with a set of wings. Boots suggested they name their new club the Hells Angels after the patch, and they went to a local trophy shop and had a set of patches made in April of 1957, not knowing that their actions that day would be the origin of one of the most notorious motorcycle clubs in history, one that is still going strong today.

At the time, there were numerous independent Hells Angels motorcycle clubs throughout California, often not even knowing about each other. Barger founded the Oakland Chapter of the HAMC in 1958 as president and quickly moved up the ranks to become the national president. Sonny Barger is widely credited with organizing the disparate groups under one "mothership," and for the tremendous international growth under his leadership. Barger also engineered the movement of the HAMC from crimes against public order to organized crime for profit.

Barger organized the HAMC like a traditional business with an organizational structure, including chapter and national positions of president, vice president, treasurer, intelligence officer, and sergeant at arms (security). Members pay fees, hold fundraisers, and also make money legitimately. They have trademarked their images and make a significant amount of money selling trademarked merchandise like T-shirts and other branded gear. The Hells Angels are big business, and while exact numbers are difficult to attain for obvious reasons, it is thought that worldwide revenue is in the billions of dollars.

Today the HAMC has over 2,500 members in over 200 charters across twenty-nine countries and six continents. The Hells Angels brand is so strong that they have become a business, formally incorporated in both the United States and Canada. Local, federal, and international law enforcement agencies allege that the Hells Angels are in the business of a range of illicit activities, including drug distribution, trafficking of firearms and stolen goods, prostitution, arson, robbery and other violence, extortion, and money laundering. In 2011, the State Department and the Department of Homeland Security added the Hells Angels to a list of criminal organizations that includes the Mafia, the Chinese Triads, and the Japanese syndicate Yakuza. Up until his death on June 29, 2022, of stage 4 liver cancer at the age of

83 years old, Sonny Barger remained active in the Hells Angels Cave Creek Arizona Chapter since moving there from Oakland in 1998. In typical Barger fashion, Sonny announced his own death with a pre-written Facebook post:

> *"I've lived a long and good life filled with adventure. And I've had the privilege to be part of an amazing club."*

In the interest of full disclosure, the Hells Angels claim they are just a group:

> *"of motorcycle enthusiasts who have joined to ride motorcycles together, organize social events, fundraisers, parties and motorcycle rallies."*

LESSON 17

ENCOURAGE CRITICAL THINKING AND DIVERSITY OF OPINION

"Leaders accept dissent, the tyrant goes it alone."
– Sonny Barger

Great leaders know they don't have all the answers. Sonny believed he had an obligation to the club to foster dissent and create a culture that encourages differing opinions. As strange as it sounds given the outlaw motorcycle club context, he also understood that leading a group of 1 percenters by fear and intimidation only works in the short term, which is why he was able to hold the position for five decades. By the way, the 1 percent label originated in the 1960s when the American Motorcycle Association published an article in its magazine stating "99 percent of all of their members are law-abiding citizens and only 1 percent are 'outlaws.'" Of course, the outlaw motorcycle clubs embraced this moniker and immediately began adding "1 %er" patches to their cuts (sleeveless leather jackets). One of the core leadership functions in any MC (motorcycle club) is something called "Church." When Barger would tell his VP, "Get everyone to Church," the club's leadership team would gather around a large conference table with Barger at the head.

This is where all club business is done and where decisions are made. Much discussion takes place regarding the decisions on the table, sometimes heated but always spirited. Club decisions are voted on and the majority rules; however, Sonny had the final say based on the feedback of his team.

Sonny could have easily ruled as a tyrant, but he understood that dissent and critical conflict always lead to better decisions. One of Barger's strengths was his willingness to allow this open discussion and consider the diverse perspectives of his team. Sonny often expressed the importance of personal responsibility and allowing individuals to make their own choices. He frequently stated that he didn't believe in telling his club members how to live their lives or what actions to take as long as they took responsibility for the consequences and adhered to the rules and principles of the Hells Angels. When disagreements and conflicts among members arose, Barger was known to let members resolve their differences on their own rather than intervening and imposing his decisions. This approach allowed members to learn from their mistakes and handle the consequences themselves.

In any business organization, a leadership mistake may result in a financial loss, product failure, or employee defection. In Sonny Barger's world, a leadership mistake may result in people dying. These kinds of stakes certainly come with their own set of elevated pressures and challenges, and businesses can take a lesson from Barger's masterful leadership under extreme conditions.

Many leaders surround themselves with extremely bright and loyal followers who either are uncomfortable with disagreement or have chosen sycophancy from a political standpoint. Truly great leaders have the courage and confidence to surround themselves with the most honest. Autocrats are always right because they insist they are. They rarely listen to anyone other than themselves anyway. Leaders listen and act accordingly. We are taught that conflict is bad and should be avoided, and most certainly conflict can be destructive and create dysfunction in an organization. However, an environment that encourages new ideas, viewpoints, and constructive criticism can turn conflict into a very powerful decision-making tool. This is not to say that a leader will always, or even occasionally, heed the advice of trusted advisors, but a great leader will welcome this discussion as a means to make the best possible decision for the organization.

What frequently happens is that in the course of a healthy discussion with constructive dissent, differing perspectives will organically generate thoughts and ideas that would not have occurred to anyone on their own.

LESSONS IN ACTION

This particular lesson took me quite a while to appreciate, and it began early in my leadership journey, even though I didn't know it at the time. I was a supervisor in a small manufacturing shop in the Midwest, running several departments. I joined the company with significant experience in both the industry and management. This background fostered the belief that I did have all the answers, which led to embracing an autocratic management style.

I'll never forget this story. My senior department lead was a woman named Ruby, a tough-as-nails gal who had worked there for thirty-five years and was one of the best operators I had ever worked with. I don't remember the specifics, but I had given Ruby a list of jobs that needed to get done one day and when I came back later to check on them, not a single one had been completed. When I questioned Ruby, she told me some unexpected hot jobs had come into the department and she re-prioritized my list. Of course, she was right, but my ego felt my authority was being questioned, and I said, "Ruby, you just need to learn to follow directions." Ruby looked me straight in the eye and said, "Steve, maybe you need to listen to us more often." It didn't sink in at the time, I think I said, "Yeah, yeah, whatever, just follow my instructions next time," but years later Ruby's words would play a major role in my leadership development.

Great leaders understand that their team members may have different perspectives, experiences, and expertise. By acknowledging that they don't have all the answers, they create an environment that encourages diverse thinking and welcomes contributions from others. Foster an atmosphere where respectful disagreement is encouraged and teach individuals to engage in constructive debates, focusing on ideas rather than personal attacks. Encourage the consideration of counterarguments and the exploration of different perspectives. I would come to painfully learn that an autocratic style can work in the short term with direct reports but not so much as I moved up in management and needed to get the cooperation of others outside my control. I knew I needed to make changes, but didn't know what or how. What I didn't understand at the time was that there was a very big difference between a manager and a leader. A manager does things right while a leader does the right things. You see, I had become a good manager but was nowhere near being a leader.

TAKEAWAYS

Create an environment that encourages constructive dissent. Don't confuse honest dissent with disloyalty or subversion and accept genuine dissent and criticism as it's intended and learn from it.

Understand that harmony is overrated. Diversity of opinion makes us smarter while groupthink makes us dumber. In this case 1 + 1 = 3.

Embrace conflict. It is an unavoidable part of human nature. Great leaders manage conflict to drive positive organizational improvement.

Listen first, talk second. Ask for advice when you need it, and listen when it is offered. Exercise an open mind and use the Socratic method to encourage critical thinking.

LESSON 18

CREATE AN ENVIRONMENT OF EMPOWERMENT

"We learn from our mistakes, pure and simple. Most of us can only improve after we know what it feels like to have screwed up. You have to give your people the freedom to screw up."
– Sonny Barger

Giving your people the freedom to screw up may seem like an odd statement coming from the leader of a band of hardened bikers, but Sonny understood that ruling with an iron fist and instilling the fear of failure just wouldn't work. Whether you are leading a group of tough and violent bikers or a team of factory workers, to be productive and creative, people need the freedom to make their own decisions, even when they are wrong. Sonny saw failure as an operational breakdown with only two outcomes: continued failure or improvement through learning from the mistake. Expecting his people to always agree with his vision is not empowerment; it is called politics, and it is counterproductive. Barger played a crucial role in creating a strong sense of brotherhood and camaraderie within the Hells Angels. By fostering a tight-knit community and promoting loyalty among members, he created an environment where individuals felt a sense of belonging and empowerment through their association with the club. Barger also emphasized the importance of individuality and personal freedom within the Hells Angels by encouraging members to express themselves authentically. This allowed individuals to embrace their unique identities and find empowerment through self-expression.

Sonny was a seasoned leader who understood running an organization through fear and an iron fist just doesn't work. It doesn't work in any setting, be it a traditional business, with your family, or an outlaw motorcycle club. Nothing good comes from a climate of fear; it breeds distrust, backstabbing, and worse, mutiny. The mutiny comes when someone else comes along with a better definition of fear. Sonny certainly had an ego, and a big one, but he didn't let it consume him and dictate his leadership style. He didn't want an organization in which mistakes were punished and ridiculed; he knew that just doesn't work. Sonny learned that by showing respect and allowing the freedom to screw up once in a while, the screw-ups will decline and performance will increase. As strange as it sounds in this setting, Sonny kept control of one of the biggest, baddest groups of people for over five decades by creating a culture that allowed failure as long as it came with learning.

LESSONS IN ACTION

My empowerment "Ah-Ha" moment came years later when I was interviewing for an executive position with a competitor of my current company. This position was with one division of a very large organization and the CEO of the mothership would be performing the interview as this position reported directly to him. This was an impressive businessman; he had a PhD, MBA, and was the leader of one of the largest multi-divisional companies in Wisconsin. As I was guided into his impressively large office for introductions, I stuck my hand out and said, "I truly appreciate this opportunity Dr. Sterner, I am —" and he stopped me right there and said, "Steve, please call me Frank. Titles don't mean a whole lot around here; results do." As I began to sit down in front of his massive desk, he said, "Why don't we go over here and chat?" and led me over to a small, round table with two chairs where we talked for over an hour. I left that meeting reflecting on the fact that this important businessman took the time to make sure I knew he valued my time as much as his, and that at least for that hour, we were equals (even though we clearly weren't).

Frank's values of empowerment, teamwork, and mutual respect permeated that company, and I got a hands-on education in just how powerful empowerment can be. The culture encouraged creativity and risk as long as it was in the name of improvement. Mistakes were not treated in a punitive manner but as a learning experience that was discussed in a team environment to collectively get down to the root cause and solution. Decisions were made in a team setting, again the goal was to consider the various thoughts, opinions, and perspectives of the team members. Replacing individual achievement (and failure) with a team environment results in better decisions. And as Ruby's words from years earlier came back to me, I began my transition from manager to leader.

TAKEAWAYS

Focus on results, not just actions. People must be made to feel like owners and entrepreneurs of their process, project, etc. Challenge your employees, align on objectives, then get out of their way.

Use failure as a learning opportunity. Don't just celebrate success, also celebrate the employees who failed but took a calculated risk. Demonstrate the *calculated* risk-taking behavior you want your teams to emulate.

Give credit where credit is due. Taking credit for other's accomplishments will destroy an empowering environment. Transparency and trust build the foundation for an empowered environment.

Develop an empowering leadership style. One that nurtures, coaches, mentors, encourages and supports, even (especially) in difficult situations. Don't micromanage; encourage empowerment but require accountability.

STEVE JOBS

ON CHANGING THE WORLD
1955-2011

Steve Jobs may seem like a curious choice given the "notorious" theme of the book, and Apple's founder and CEO would most certainly be at the top of my list of the greatest leaders in history as well. However, it takes very little Google effort to find countless examples that Jobs could be every bit as cruel and merciless as he was brilliant. As a tremendous Steve Jobs and Apple fan, I have to acknowledge that in the context of leadership, there was definitely a "good Steve" and a "bad Steve." The latter earned Steve Jobs's inclusion in this book.

Adopted at birth in San Francisco on February 24, 1955, Jobs is widely recognized as a pioneer of the computer revolution of the 1970s, along with Apple co-founder Steve Wozniak. Jobs co-founded Apple in 1976 with Wozniak to sell Wozniak's Apple I personal computer, which was the start of the computing revolution. Apple was literally started in Jobs's garage, coming from the printed circuit industry I find it fascinating that the first printed circuit board Wozniak built was with a piece of wood, nails for the connections, and wire for the circuits! The early computing products were the Apple I, Apple II, Apple III, the Lisa, and the first Macintosh. What happened *NeXT* is right out of a movie script. In 1985, when John Scully and the Apple board forced Jobs out of his own company, he quickly moved on and founded his next company, NeXT. Jobs then bought the computing division of George Lucas's ILM and incorporated it as Pixar. Right after *Toy Story* was released, Pixar went public, and Jobs's net worth soared to $1.5 billion, much more than at any of his time with Apple. The operating system he developed at NeXT earned Jobs the award of "Entrepreneur of the Decade" by *Inc. Magazine*. Apple, having lost the magic once Jobs left, bought NeXT in 1997 for its operating system and Jobs was quickly back running Apple. This launched the Think Different rebirth of Apple which would lead to some of the most amazing products in history: the iPod, iPhone, iTunes, iPad, MacBook, and the Apple Watch.

Side note: While I never had the pleasure of meeting Steve Jobs, I did get to spend some time with his counterpart Steve Wozniak. I speak at an annual industry conference, and one year "Woz," as he liked to be called, was the keynote speaker talking about his new book titled, of course, iWoz. After his talk attendees had the opportunity to buy the book and stand in line for an autograph and a few minutes with the man. I am a bit of a collector of autographed books, photos, movie posters, etc. and I can say that the Woz was the most gracious, down-to-earth celebrity I have ever met. The line for autographs was over 500 people, but Woz would spend as much time with each person as they wanted. When my time finally came up, I had one thing I wanted to tell him and also one question (I had had plenty of time to come up with these).

1. *The thing I wanted him to know was that both my wife Nancy and I were both huge fans of his, but for two very different reasons. I mentioned that my wife became a fan during his time on one of her favorite shows, Dancing with the Stars, and then I stated that of course I was a fan of his technological genius.*

2. *The question I asked him was, "How did you and Steve pick the name Apple for your company?" Woz replied that he didn't believe he had ever been asked this question before and then he relayed a story that Jobs had told him after he asked the same question. The story goes that Jobs was visiting a relative and filling him in on this exciting new company he and Woz were creating when the relative asked what the name of the company was. Jobs replied, "We haven't decided yet," and as the two looked at each other standing in the middle of an apple orchard the relative owned, each munching on an apple, Jobs said, "What about Apple, it's not intimidating and is kind of fun?" This may also explain the Apple logo with the bite out of it. And the rest, as they say, is history!*

By the way, the autograph by Woz in the book reads, "To Nancy, Keep watching Dancing With the Stars, Woz."

There have been many urban legends about the naming of the company, from Jobs wanting Apple to be listed ahead of his former employer Atari in the phone book, to being a tribute to Alan Turing, the father of theoretical computer science and AI who died after biting into an apple laced with cyanide. I prefer to go with the story told to me by one of the only two people in the world that really knew.

It is a rare person who can look back on their life and say, "I changed the world"; Steve Jobs was one of those people. It staggers the mind to think that he literally touched nearly every single person on the planet in some way, shape, or form with his visionary products that redefined the computer, music, and movie industries. Jobs knew what we needed and wanted before we ever did, by not only listening to his customers, but also by interpreting what customers were saying. For example, Henry Ford's customers wanted to get from Point A to Point B faster, but if he had asked them what they wanted, they would have told him "a faster horse." Jobs's genius was in anticipating customer needs, distilling them to the basic level, and then developing products that exceeded those core needs. With his death from pancreatic cancer at the age of fifty-six in 2011, perhaps there may never be another business leader like him. One day soon, the name Jobs will replace Einstein when people are comparing genius by saying: "He was the Jobs of our generation."

LESSON 19

KEEP IT SIMPLE

---

*"That's been one of my mantras — focus and simplicity.
Simple can be harder than complex; you have to work hard to
get your thinking clean to make it simple."*
– Steve Jobs

Every one of Apple's revolutions was born of the company's devotion to simplicity. Each new device either created a new category or turned an existing category on its head—all because, as an old iMac ad put it, the technology was "simply amazing, and amazingly simple." Steve Jobs's belief in the power of simplicity of design was never more apparent than with the three consumer-device home runs he created in the early 2000s: the iPod, iPhone, and iPad. Jobs immersed himself daily in the design of the original iPod and its interface. His main demand was "Simplify!" As he brought up each screen, he would apply a typical Steve Jobs test: everything should be able to be accessed with three clicks or less, and the clicks should be intuitive. If Jobs couldn't figure out how to navigate to something, or if it took more than three clicks, he would be brutal with the design team. Tony Fadell, the iPod team leader Jobs hired specifically for that product, recounted a typical Steve Jobs intervention: "There would be times when we'd rack our brains on a user interface problem and think we'd considered every option, and he would go, 'Did you think of this?' He'd redefine the problem or approach, and our little problem would go away."

Ken Segall, creative director at Apple's longtime ad agency, shared the following personal story illustrating Jobs's obsession with simplicity.

> *While at dinner with Internet browser pioneer Marc Andreessen in 2006, Jobs pulled his personal prototype iPhone out of his jeans pocket and said to Andreessen, "Here, let me show you something," and walked him through all of the features and capabilities of the new device. After the appropriate amount of oohing and aahing over Jobs's new vision, BlackBerry aficionado Andreessen asked Jobs, "Boy, Steve, don't you think it's going to be a problem not having a physical keyboard? Are people going to be OK typing directly on the screen?" Jobs looked Andreessen right in the eye with that piercing gaze and said, "They'll get used to it." Apple sold 1.4 million iPhones in the first year, and as of the date of this book has sold over 2 billion. Once again, Jobs was right.*

Apple's package design team had just returned from their presentation to Steve Jobs, and their faces told the story. While there were no visible signs of carnage, the team just had that "things didn't go exactly as we planned" look. Ken felt bad for them because he knew they'd been pouring their hearts into a project for several weeks, trying to solve a thorny packaging issue. Ken was working on an unrelated project in the building and had been invited into their high-security, hermetically sealed chamber at several points to join the brainstorming. While the team was decompressing after their Steve meeting, he crossed paths with the project leader in the creative group's kitchen. "The suspense is killing me," he said. "How'd it go this morning?" The team leader said, "Well, Steve hit us with the Simple Stick." Translation: Steve had rejected their work—not because it was bad, but because in some way it failed to distill the idea to its essence. It took a turn when it should have traveled a straight line.

In this case, it hadn't even been the creative effort that bothered Steve; it was the project itself. The person leading the project had directed the team to create packaging for two versions of the same product. Steve had decided this was brain-dead and said, "Just combine them, one product, one box." There was no need to explore the idea of a second package. He was right. It was simpler, quicker, better. The conversation was over in minutes, and it left one very smart and talented group of people wondering why they hadn't thought of that themselves.

The Simple Stick symbolizes a core value within Apple. Sometimes it's held up as inspiration; other times it's wielded like a caveman's club. In all cases, it's a reminder of what sets Apple apart from other technology companies and what makes Apple stand out in a complicated world: a deep, almost religious belief in the power of simplicity.

LESSONS IN ACTION

I still remember the day I was driving home and heard the news on the radio that Steve Jobs had passed. My immediate reaction was sadness, and although the public nature of his illness prevented this news from being a complete surprise, I was still sad. And although I have admired him as a charismatic leader for a very long time, I think I have admired him more for his visionary innovation. Part of my sadness was purely selfish; I was sad for all of us who could not get through a single day without using one of his incredible products and wondered if this was the end of Apple's innovation revolution. His genius was developing products that outperformed the competition while making them sexy and fun. The iFamily of products are so intuitive they don't have a user manual. By just playing around with one for ten minutes, you can become not only functional but fairly well-versed in the device. I remember being very resistant early on in the iPod craze, and my first couple of MP3 players were extremely limited, difficult to use, and just plain ugly. When I finally converted and bought my first iPod, I was in awe of the simplicity, technology, and "coolness" of the device. The initial "click wheel" was so far ahead of the competition, it was absolute genius.

My approach, in fact, the foundation of the services of my consulting company, is based on Jobs's single-minded philosophy that "Simple is Better." However, anyone who has ever gone down this path quickly realizes that simple is not only better, it's harder, much harder! Whether it is business practices, quality systems, or customer relations, over time companies almost always end up making things much more complex than is necessary. I think what Steve was talking about is that the "design" of a system is harder when the goal is to make the product or service simple and easy for the end user. Over time, a company's Business Management System (BMS) documentation becomes bloated, overgrown, and ineffective. What typically happens is that with every customer complaint and external audit, things get added to the system in a knee-jerk reaction and the documentation set grows and grows and grows until it is an unrecognizable, big, hairy monster. When I engage with a new client, we first go through a discovery phase where we review together every process with a critical eye aimed at three questions:

1. Does this activity add value to the organization?

2. Is this process working the way you want it to?

3. How can we simplify the process and increase the value to the organization?

During this discovery phase, it is not uncommon to find forty-plus high-level procedures, three times as many transactional work instructions, and hundreds of forms. It is also typical to find many of these documents to be over twenty pages long, begging the question: "Is anyone going to read and use a twenty-page work instruction?" I suggest a resounding "NO." So, if that is true, what is the point? Procedures and work instructions need to be user-friendly: clear, concise, and as brief as possible while remaining functional. The magic, and difficulty, is to make the complex simple. This requires a particular skill set and a vast knowledge of management systems and customer expectations. The results from a recent project resulted in a seventy-eight percent reduction in the amount of documentation, which is pretty typical with my projects. Simple IS better.

TAKEAWAYS

Embrace Occam's Razor. A Franciscan friar from the 14th century named William of Ockham had it right; simple is better.

Learn From Your Kids. Children usually choose the path of least resistance and don't read user manuals. Whatever it is, make it intuitively obvious and easy to use.

Making It Simple Is Iterative. When you get something to the point of acceptable simplicity, start over and make it simpler.

Understand The Complexity Ratio. There is a direct correlation between complexity and the chance someone will screw it up. Simplicity is not about what you lose, but what you gain.

LESSON 20

BE A HERETIC

---

*"Here's to the crazy ones, the misfits, the rebels, the troublemakers,
the round pegs in the square holes . . . The ones who see things
differently—they're not fond of rules . . . You can quote them, disagree
with them, glorify or vilify them, but the only thing you can't do is
ignore them because they change things . . . They push the human race
forward, and while some may see them as the crazy ones, we see
genius, because the ones who are crazy enough to think that they
can change the world, are the ones who do."*
– Steve Jobs

What is a heretic? In this context, it is a person who has opinions, ideas, and perspectives that are in direct opposition to the current "organizational norms"; they challenge everything and don't accept "This is the way we have always done it." The truly great leaders are heretics; they challenge the status quo, develop solutions, and drive change. Being a heretic is not for the weak; they are often (almost always) ridiculed, criticized, and not taken seriously— at first. Heretics don't follow, they lead.

One of the greatest heretics of all time—and one of my personal favorites—was Steve Jobs. He had the incredible vision to create products that people didn't even know they wanted until they saw them! Designing products that are beautiful, simple, and intuitive shattered the cookie-cutter products of Apple's competition. One story that illustrates Jobs's penchant for shattering the status quo comes during the early development of the iPhone.

Jobs changed the face of product design, and his pursuit of "elegance" was not limited to the outside of a device. He was famously obsessed with making the inside of devices simple and uncluttered even though the consumer would never see it. This was a lesson he learned early in life from his father, who once told him: "When you're a carpenter making a beautiful chest of drawers, you're not going to use a piece of plywood on the back, even though it faces the wall and nobody will ever see it. You'll know it's there, so you're going to use a beautiful piece of wood in the back. For you to sleep well at night, the aesthetic, the quality, has to be carried all the way through." This lesson would stay with Jobs his entire life and form the foundation for his obsession with design elegance.

Steve Jobs and Apple turned several industries on their heads, but perhaps none more than the music industry. Kids today cannot imagine the sheer joy my generation got from spending Saturday afternoons in the local record store filing through racks and racks of vinyl LP albums. They would not believe we would gladly pay $10-$15 to purchase a twelve-song album when we only wanted one or two of the twelve songs.

I still remember the frustration of being in the car jamming to a tune on my state-of-the-art 8-track player only to hear the familiar fade-out, click, and fade-in as the song moved from one track to the next. Cassettes were a bit better, but both tapes could be easily demagnetized which would erase the songs. We all thought we had reached music nirvana when the CD was introduced and we could instantly change songs without having to fast-forward through the ones before it. This was just the way it was, and nobody questioned it. Well, nobody until Steve Jobs.

Music became portable with the introduction of the 8-track, cassette tapes, and finally CDs, but you still had to buy the entire song list. CDs were more durable than tapes and provided a skip-free listening experience, and also divided the audiophile community into the vinyl purists vs. the digital aficionados. The purists prefer the snap, crackle, and pop of vinyl albums while the digital fans love the clean, crisp digital sound of the CD. I remember spending youthful hours using a piezoelectric gun to reduce static electricity before and applying a protective coating afterward to protect my vinyl albums from wear. I also put my albums in clear protective sleeves. My family thought I was crazy. CDs were fantastic, but technology never stands still and they didn't solve the issue of having to buy the entire album (CD) of songs whether you liked them all or not.

As technology stands still for nobody, Apple recently eliminated the need to purchase songs altogether by piggybacking onto popular video streaming services and launching Apple Music, a music streaming service that gives users access to unlimited songs through a monthly service subscription. Users can play playlists they create or simply use their voice-activated speakers and say, "Alexa (or Siri or Hey Google), play 'Friends in Low Places'" or "play Jelly Roll" to hear a nonstop playlist of his songs. Even though Apple Music was launched four years after the death of Jobs, you can bet he somehow had his fingers in the concept that once again kept Apple an industry leader in another new market.

LESSONS IN ACTION

Many organizations I work with are focused on maintaining the status quo, a place full of workers who are fearful of change of any kind. These are cultures that want to keep things stable, comfortable, and predictable and get freaked out when a unicorn shows up at the door and rocks the boat. A unicorn is anything or anyone that disrupts the status quo in an organization, even though everyone knows the status quo "sucks." The average "unenlightened" factory in our business is fraught with anxiety and short-term fixes that perpetuate the status quo. How much time does the average manager spend "firefighting" instead of moving the business forward? Too much, I would argue, and spending your time putting out fires is extremely exhausting. Does this sound familiar? If not, good for you, however, you are probably in the minority.

These companies have what I call a sheepwalking culture. The term *sheep* is often viewed as a negative when applied to people, but in this context, I am referring to behavior, blindly following something simply because it is the "way we have always done things," in other words, sheepwalking. I would bet a boatload of beer that at some time in your career a boss has told you something like: "Be a good soldier and just do what I say; you have to be a team player and take one for the team." Many times we do something we know is not the right thing to do because we don't want to rock the boat, cause issues, or put a bull's-eye on our backs. This is the behavior of the sheep. I don't blame the sheep; I blame the leadership. This disruptive leadership is not limited to business, perhaps the most pervasive sheepwalking comes from the leaders of our educational system. From elementary school through university, indoctrination is the norm and critical thinking is often squashed. Teaching and graduating sheep is a lot easier than developing students to think for themselves and question the status quo. IMHO, the reason we rank so low in world academic achievement is the fact that we graduate so many sheep. Well-educated sheep, but compliant, color-inside-the-lines followers, nonetheless.

Do the names "Rio" or "MPMan" sound familiar? Probably not, unless you owned one (I owned a Rio). Before 2001, they were part of the first MP3 players to hit the market. Back then, you either had to rip a CD or download bootlegged music files to get them on the player, and capacity was only about twenty songs. Where others may have seen a crowded market, Jobs realized this as a market opportunity and introduced the iPod in 2001 with Steve Jobs's jaw-dropping statement at the product launch of "1,000 songs in your pocket." At a time when space was at a premium, the iPod simplified access to music and data storage and truly revolutionized how we listen to music.

The next genius Jobs move was to redefine how we purchase music; he saw an opportunity where no one else did. There were some early peer-to-peer (bootleg) music-sharing websites like Napster and Limewire where you could download digital songs, but the quality was awful. People would post songs that they had converted from a turntable or CD or had recorded the song by placing a microphone in front of a speaker that was playing it. After the recording industry sued Napster in 2002 for copyright infringement, it virtually locked CDs with digital rights management to prevent the sharing of music. This got Jobs's attention, and the only reason iTunes exists today is Napster. Being the heretic he was, Jobs recognized that music fans wanted an easy, affordable, and legal way to download only the songs that they liked instead of driving to the local record store for an album or CD. Jobs worked with record label executives and major recording artists to pitch his vision and iTunes was released in 2003 with a price of 99 cents per song.

Some major artists initially refused to allow their music to be sold on iTunes; however, they quickly realized that they could make way more money by selling billions of single songs for 99 cents each globally than through thousands of vinyl albums and CDs locally. In its first week, iTunes sold one million downloads and quickly became not only the top online music retailer but also displaced the brick-and-mortar retail outlets, propelling Apple into one of the biggest companies in the world.

Heretics lead, sheep follow. We need more heretics. Leadership is hard, but what's harder is finding the strength to become a heretic, to drive radical change in the face of massive resistance and to inspire others to break the norm and do the same. The world needs more Steve Jobses, people who have a vision and can create ways to bust through the stagnant cultures entrenched in our businesses.

TAKEAWAYS

Remember, it was heretics that discovered the world is not flat. Ignore the people that say you're crazy; they just don't have the vision, or courage, to challenge the norms.

Think differently. Reward "unlike" thinking; create a culture that rewards ideas and act upon them. Set the example; critical thinking is contagious.

Be a rule breaker. Heretics know the rules better than the rule makers; become an expert at the rules and then break them with innovation and creativity.

Change the game. To be in the top one percent you have to be willing to do what the other ninety-nine percent won't. The world has enough sheep.

EPILOGUE

I hope you have enjoyed reading *Notorious* as much as I enjoyed writing it. Any historical errors are mine and mine alone. The twenty business lessons presented in the book are solid business practices, and I hope you have found at least a few of these that can be applied immediately to improve your leadership and business. From leadership lessons in strategy and power to organizational culture and marketing, there are lessons here for everyone.

The *Lessons in Action* illustrate each lesson with real-life failures and successes from my personal leadership journey. Learn from both.

The *Takeaways* that accompany each lesson are words of wisdom that hopefully will provide you with practical philosophies that can be applied immediately.

The true student of leadership will care less about where the lessons come from and more about what they can learn from them and apply to their advantage. In today's business environment, we all need every advantage we can get.

Thanks for reading.

Steve

ACKNOWLEDGMENTS

Of course, I must begin by acknowledging the cast of characters that inspired this book: Sun Tzu, Attila the Hun, Freydis Eiriksdottir, Genghis Khan, Blackbeard the Pirate, Catherine the Great, Napoleon Bonaparte, Al Capone, Sonny Barger, and Steve Jobs. Without their exploits and adventures, there would be no book.

For historical background on the subjects, many thanks to the resources of History.com, Wikipedia-History.com, The Biography Channel, and the Ancient History Encyclopedia.

Natasha Lyn Lehndorf for her design and graphic creative genius, countless hours, and patience corralling all of my incoherent ideas into amazing art and illustrations.

Atmosphere Press for taking a chance on Notorious and providing exceptional editing, creative, and publishing resources.

A very special thanks to Jack Canfield for writing the foreword. Jack's Chicken Soup books have sold over 500 million copies. I developed a relationship with Jack during one of his Author's Mastermind Retreats. Jack's guidance and mentorship were invaluable in recrafting this 2nd edition of Notorious.

And finally, many, many thanks to my family for tolerating the long days and nights researching and writing, taking away from our limited family time. Special thanks to Nancy and Morgan for being my sanity check and overall sounding board.

ABOUT ATMOSPHERE PRESS

Founded in 2015, Atmosphere Press was built on the principles of Honesty, Transparency, Professionalism, Kindness, and Making Your Book Awesome. As an ethical and author-friendly hybrid press, we stay true to that founding mission today.

If you're a reader, enter our giveaway for a free book here:

SCAN TO ENTER
BOOK GIVEAWAY

If you're a writer, submit your manuscript for consideration here:

SCAN TO SUBMIT
MANUSCRIPT

And always feel free to visit Atmosphere Press and our authors online at atmospherepress.com. See you there soon!

ABOUT THE AUTHOR

STEVE WILLIAMS has over forty-five years of experience in the electronics industry, having gained prominence and recognition as an industry authority on quality, management, and leadership throughout his career. He has held executive positions in strategic sourcing, operations, engineering, quality, and organizational excellence, and is the president and founder of *The Right Approach Consulting*. He has been a distinguished MBA faculty member at several major universities and has published over 200 white papers and articles on a variety of business topics. He is a frequent public speaker and has dedicated his career to helping companies improve operational performance. *Notorious* is his sixth book, with two of his prior books receiving critical acclaim as a must-read across the industry.

Steve lives in Wisconsin with his wife, Nancy, and very spoiled puppies, Savvi and Daisy.